P9-EED-500

AVIAT...

...BLE SUR LA NAVIGATION AÉRIENNE SANS BALLONS

M. le Dr HUREAU DE VILLENEUVE

...vements de mécanique, pour faciliter les Études

Nota. — Les appareils précédés du signe * ont été construits et expérimentés.

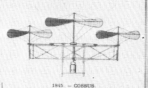

...D. — Appareil ... d'un ... pour amortir ...

* 1784. — LAUNOY et BIENVENU. — Premier hélicoptère présenté à l'Académie des Sciences, composé de deux hélices tournant en sens inverse sous l'effort d'un arc de baleine.

* 1806. — Jacob DEGEN. — Système d'ailes formant parachute. Cet appareil n'ayant pu s'enlever, l'auteur y ajouta par la suite, un petit ballon.

1842. — HENSON. — Système de plan incliné, monté sur roues. Les hélices sont actionnées par une machine à vapeur.

1845. — COSSUS. — Appareil composé d'hélices ascensionnelles mues par la vapeur.

1856. — Viscount CARLINGFORD. — Genre d'aéroplane monté sur roues, possédant une hélice et une queue mobile.

1857. — LE BRIS. — L'auteur produisait l'abaissement des ailes à l'aide de leviers; des ressorts aidaient à les relever.

1857. — Du TEMPLE. — Disposition d'aéroplane monté sur roues, avec un hélice à l'avant actionnée par la vapeur.

1859. — BRIGHT. — Système composé d'hélices ascensionnelles tournant en sens inverse.

— De GROOF. — Appareil composé de trois leviers, et dans lequel l'auteur ...

1864. — STRUVE et TELESCHEFF. — Ailes mues par la force humaine agissant sur un ressort.

1864. — CLAUDEL. — Aéronef orthoptère. Système d'ailes tournantes actionnées par la vapeur.

* 1866. — BOURCART. — Appareil mû par les pieds. Dans cette disposition, l'aile se présente en tranchant pendant son relèvement, et à plat pendant son abaissement.

* 1867. — Le BRIS. — Les ailes sont fixes, mais leur orientation convenable force l'appareil à s'enlever.

* 1871. — DANJARD. — Appareil formant parachute composé de deux ailes propulsives et d'une hélice, le tout mû par la force humaine.

1871. — POMÈS et de la PAUZE. — Appareil pourvu d'un gouvernail et d'une hélice, actionnée par un moteur à poudre.

* 1871. — Thomas MOY. — Système d'aéroplane monté sur roues et dont les hélices sont mises en mouvement par une machine à vapeur.

* 1871. — PÉNAUD. — Premier aéroplane de l'auteur, dit planophore, composé de plans à bords relevés et d'une hélice mue par la torsion du caoutchouc. Cet appareil, qui peut monter ou descendre suivant la position de son centre de gravité, a pu franchir 60 m. en 13 secondes.

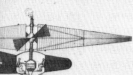

— Machine volante composée d'une hélice d'ascension, d'une d'avapeur qui fait mouvoir les hélices agit directement sur ces dern...

1876. — PÉNAUD et GAUCHOT. — Système d'aéroplane à vapeur pourvu d'hélices, d'un gouvernail et de roulettes à pattes flexibles.

* 1877. — E. DIEUAIDE. — Expérience sur l'hélice au moyen d'un tube flexible amenant la vapeur d'une chaudière fixe. L'hélice double ne paraît pas susceptible, à cause de la perte due aux engrenages, d'une force ascensionnelle de plus de 12 kilogrammes par cheval-vapeur.

1877. — MÉLIKOFF. — Hélicoptère à vapeur d'hélice. L'hélice est disposée pour former parachute.

* 1879. — BREAREY. — Système d'ailes flexibles mues par la ... L'appareil est monté sur roues, et son centre de gravité est ta... pour l'ascension ou la descente.

* 1879. — TATIN. — Aéroplane à air comprimé monté sur roues et expérimenté à Meudon. À une vitesse de 8 mètres par seconde, cet appareil quitte le sol.

* 1879. — DANDRIEUX. — Appareil disposé pour obtenir un allégement sur place. Les ailes se meuvent suivant un axe oblique, et le mouvement qu'elles font est à peu près celui du chiffre 8.

1880. — EDISON. — Projet d'un grand navire aérien pour faire le tour du monde. L'appareil est monté sur roues et les ailes sont mues par un moteur.

...pour arriver au but; cependant, la difficulté qu'on ...ptement le centre de gravité, oblige à rechercher un ...st probable que le premier appareil d'aviation qui ...es ou autres organes intermédiaires, soustrayant une

E. D.

E. DIEUAIDE, 18, Rue de la Banque. — PARIS.

Bureau pour les BREVETS, DESSINS, CONSTRUCTION D'APPAREILS

...du Caire, 95-97.

1-16-75

Flight before Flying

Also by David Wragg
World's Air Forces
A Dictionary of Aviation
Speed in the Air

Flight before Flying

David W. Wragg

A World of Books That Fill a Need

Frederick Fell Publishers, Inc.   New York

Manufactured and first published in England by:
Osprey Publishing Ltd.
707 Oxford Road
Reading, Berkshire

Designed by Behram Kapadia
Filmset and printed by BAS Printers Limited,
Wallop, Hampshire

For information address:
Frederick Fell Publishers, Inc.
386 Park Avenue South
New York, N.Y. 10016

Library of Congress Catalog Card No. 73-93897

In Canada:
George J. McLeod, Limited
Toronto 2B, Ontario

International Standard Book Number 0-8119-0233-1

Contents

Introduction

Popular history tends to be highly selective – only the first person to perform a particular feat, and only the major achievements are remembered by most people. Something of this is inevitable, and *Flight before Flying* has no pretensions towards being a detailed record of every move made by even the most obscure of the early aeronauts. But it is an attempt to give the period which ended with the historic flight of Orville Wright far more attention than it usually gets, and it is hoped that it will draw the attention of a wide readership to the successes and failures which accompanied the development of the aeroplane. With the help of more than 150 illustrations I have tried to convey some of the interest and excitement of the pre-aeroplane days in a way which treads the narrow line between being merely factual on the one hand, or flippant on the other.

I should also like to take this opportunity of thanking those who have helped towards the accumulation of the material which is so important for a work of this kind, not least being those in the museums, libraries and institutions which have assisted with the illustrations, and in particular I should like to mention Miss F. Vaughan of the Science Museum, Miss Catherine Scott of the Smithsonian Institution, and Lieutenant-Colonel J.B. Reveilhac of the Musée de l'Air.

David W. Wragg
April, 1973

Chapter 1

IN THE BEGINNING

Myth and legend, kites, windmills, tower jumpers,
ornithopters, first theories, helicopter toys, Da Vinci,
parachute designs, predictions, earthbound flying-machines.

*'If the heavens then be penetrable, and no
lets, it were not amiss to make wings
and fly up; and some new-fangled wits,
methinks, should some time or other
find out.'*

ROBERT BURTON, 1621

Man has seldom been satisfied to rest content with his achievements. He has devoted an inordinate amount of time and energy throughout history in striving to be the master of his surroundings, and not always for practical and necessary reasons of survival. No one can be sure when the idea of flight first occurred to Man, largely because of the romance with which flight has been surrounded through the ages and which has given this aspect of history a more generous helping of myth and legend than has been accorded to more mundane matters. From ancient Egypt come illustrations of winged gods, from Assyria, the winged bull, from Greece the winged horse, Pegasus, and from Rome, the god Mercury. Some people have even tried to link the early legends with space flight in an attempt to explain the gaps in the story of man's evolution.

For many, the story of flight begins with the legend of Daedalus and his son, Icarus, from classical mythology. Daedalus, an architect who constructed the Cretan labyrinth, was imprisoned by King Minos on the island and flight was his sole means of escape. Daedalus made wings from bird feathers and wax for himself and his son. After Daedalus had warned his son not to fly too close to the sun, for fear of melting the wax, they took off for Sicily with the wings attached to their arms. Unfortunately, Icarus ignored his father's advice and fell to his death, although Daedalus is supposed to have landed safely in Sicily – all in all, a most unlikely achievement.

The Macedonian, Alexander the Great, according to legend, journeyed to view the heavens in a chariot drawn by gryphons – winged beasts of mythology – who were encouraged to this effort by pieces of meat placed just out of their reach. Even in England, there is the legend of King Bladud, who is supposed to have attempted to fly over London in 852 BC, but fell to his death. Before this, King Kai Kawus of Persia is supposed to have made a legendary flight in 1500 BC in a chariot drawn by eagles. Slightly more credible is the story of the Chinese Emperor Shin who, in 2200 BC, is supposed to have jumped from a tower and glided safely to the ground using two large reed mats. One could in fact credit Shin with being the first of the tower jumpers – who are sometimes thought to be a medieval European phenomenon.

On a more definite note, Hero of Alexandria, some 2,000 years ago, discovered the propulsive effects of a jet of steam, designing a rotating boiler which, when suspended above a fire, rotated as the steam escaped from four nozzles.

It is possible to disregard such items as the boomerang, the arrow and the throwing spear from any study of the evolution of flight, since these are in effect unpowered projectiles, lacking controlled flight or man-carrying potential. The next significant development must be the kite, of which the origins are lost in the mists of antiquity. It is known, however, that kites originated in China, and gradually found their way to Europe, taking some 2,000 years to arrive by the thirteenth century. Initially, the kite was used as a plaything in Europe, although the ancient Chinese are known to have built man-carrying kites, probably BC, and the early kite was usually dragon-shaped, the familiar plane surface and diamond-shaped kite not becoming known until the fifteenth century.

The kite was not the only item of aeronautical significance to be relegated to the status of plaything during the period in question. The airscrew or propeller made its appearance as the windmill during the thirteenth century, before appearing as a toy, either a string-pull helicopter, sometimes known as a *moulinet à noix* by the French, during the fourteenth century AD, or as the simpler *moulinet à vent*, which consisted simply of an airscrew on a stick. Unlike the kite, the windmill as it is known in Europe had no Chinese counter-part – the Chinese windmills having the sails mounted horizontally, with one side of the windmill boxed in.

Even before the advent of the windmill in Europe, and while the kite was making its slow progress from the then isolated Cathay, a new era in aero-nautics was unfolding in Europe with the advent of the tower jumpers, who used either stiff cloaks or wings to attempt a glide or man-powered flight to the ground. The first recorded instance of a tower jumper in the West was that of the Moor, Armen Firman, at Cordoba in Spain in AD 852. A later attempt was by a Benedictine monk, known variously as Oliver or Eilmer of Malmesbury, who jumped from Malmesbury Abbey in 1029 after fitting himself with wings – and was lucky merely to break both legs after a short glide. Not long afterwards, the 'Saracen of Constantinople' fell to his death after jumping using a large cloak fitted with stiffeners.

An interval of some hundreds of years seems to have followed these early efforts, the next recorded instance of a tower jumping being in 1496, when a citizen of Nuremberg, Senecio, is reported to have broken an arm in an un-successful flight. Then came the Italian mathematician, Danti, in 1503, who was seriously injured after attempting to fly at Perugia with wings attached to his arms. Others followed: John Damian, the Italian-born Abbot of Tungland, was injured in a jump from Stirling Castle in 1507, and an Italian clock-maker, Bolori, was killed in 1536 while jumping from the Cathedral of Troyes in France.

The period was not entirely fruitless, although the tower jumpers might seem to suggest that it was. Mythology and legend was being replaced by imagination and fiction. A Franciscan monk, Roger Bacon (c. 1214–94) men-tioned in his work *De mirabili potestate carto et naturae*, written in 1250 and published three hundred years later in Paris, hollow globes of copper filled with 'aetherial air', capable of floating in the atmosphere, and flying-machines in which a man could sit and propel himself by working a mechanical device. Bacon's predictions were taken further by a Jesuit, Father Francesco de Lana de Terzi, in his book, *Prodromo overo Saggio*, in 1670, which included an illustration of a flying ship, supported aloft by four copper spheres emptied of air. De Lana went even further, describing aerial bombardment and assault. An illustration in 1326 by Walter de Milemetre depicted a windsock kite, with small wings, dropping a bomb over a besieged city; and another illustration, in 1420, by the Italian, Joanes Fontana, depicted a model bird with what appears to be a rocket efflux from the tail.

On a more practical level, the famous Italian Rennaissance artist, Leonardo da Vinci (1452–1519), has the credit for producing some of the first constructive and considered appraisals of the possibilities of flight, although the Da Vinci designs could hardly be described as scientific. Much of Da Vinci's work depended on inaccurate imitations of bird flight – otherwise known as ornithoptering flight – and it was not until later that the possibilities of the fixed-wing glider were taken into account. Man-power was considered by Da Vinci to be sufficient for most of his designs, with both arm and leg propulsion for the larger and heavier designs. The position of the pilot varied from the prone, with an almost 'swimming' action, to standing upright. Nevertheless, much valuable knowledge would have been gained by the early and mid-nineteenth century pioneers of flight if they had had the opportunity of studying Da Vinci's ideas. They were denied this knowledge by the incompetence and lack of imagination of his executor, which resulted in the complete neglect of his work until its eventual publication during the late nineteenth century, by which time it post-dated the valuable scientific work of Sir George Cayley and Horatio Phillips. While *Sul Volo degli Uccelli,* written in 1505, contained the great man's observations on bird flight, his other notable achievements included a pyramid-shaped parachute design, an elevator control operated by a head-harness, a form of retractable undercarriage, and a clockwork-powered helicopter, as well as a bow-string powered ornithopter. None of the designs was built, but the true genius of the man can be recognised in the fact that he also designed what in effect would have been a battle tank, some four hundred years before the appearance of this weapon.

Another design for the parachute concept came from one of Da Vinci's fellow countrymen when Fausto Veranzio published his *Machinae novae* in 1595, with the first published illustration of a parachute. Unlike Leonardo da Vinci, Veranzio based his *'homo volans'* parachute upon a ship's sail – not unnaturally, since the sight of billowing canvas must have been bound to inspire some thoughts in this direction.

Attempts to build flying-machines were made. One of the first was by Hautsch in Nuremberg during the early seventeenth century – although, in common with many during the following three hundred years, it remained firmly earthbound. A model aircraft was built at about this time by Tito Livio Burattini, who followed this with a full-size version in 1648. Using four sets of wings, with the leading and trailing sets for propulsion and the other two sets for lift, and intended to be spring-powered, the Burattini design also remained earthbound, although the working model has been credited with a short flight in some circles. Others believe that it was in fact a kite because its name, flying dragon, was an alternative name for a kite of the period.

The tower jumpers had not disappeared from the scene. One such foolhardy individual named Bernoin, was killed in 1673 while attempting to fly with wings at Frankfurt-am-Main. A French locksmith, Besnier, attempted to fly from the roof of a house at Sable in 1678, using a device worked by his feet, and managed to land without injury. The idea that the arms of a man could not provide sufficient power for flight had already occurred to Giovanni Alfonso Borelli (1608–79) in Italy and to Robert Hooke (1635–1703) in England, who had drawn attention to the differences between the muscular structure of men and birds. Hooke suggested that some form of engine would be essential, and in 1655 made a spring-powered ornithopter model which appears to have been able to move through the air. He is also believed to have produced designs, now lost, for man-carrying machines. It was another Englishman, Francis Willughby (?–1672), who suggested, in his *Ornithologiae libre tres*, published in 1676, that a man's legs, rather than his arms, were comparable in muscular strength to the wings of a bird. In spite of this, Canon Oger of Rosoy Abbey, attempted to tower jump, landing in a bush, and a priest from Peronne fell into a moat.

Strangely, it was at this time that the first science fiction seems to have appeared, although in their ignorance the authors took considerable licence with the depth of the earth's atmosphere and the gravitational pull. By coincidence, two such books were published in England in 1638. One of these was *Man in the Moone*, by the Bishop of Hereford, Francis Godwin (1562–1633), telling the story of one Gonsales who trained wild swans to carry him to the moon, while the other, by the then Bishop of Chester, John Wilkins (1614–72), *Discovery of a New World*, considered whether or not the moon might be inhabited. Other, later books by Wilkins included *Discourse concerning Flying*, published in 1640, and *Mathematical Magick*, published eight years later. The latter speculated on the means of flight, by angels, with the

12

aid of birds, with wings fastened to the body, and by flying chariots. Seemingly not to be outdone, a Jesuit, Gaspar Schott, had published in 1658 a book, *Magia universalis naturae et artis*, which in effect dealt with the possibilities of aerostation, but did not carry science forward in any way.

Cyrano de Bergerac, in 1654, had published his *Histoire comique, ou Voyage dans la Lune,* and this was translated into English in 1659. The book offered such incredible means of flight to the moon as depending on bottles of dew attached to the body, which provided lift as the sun soaked up the dew.

During the early years of the eighteenth century, a Brazilian priest, Father Laurenço de Gusmão (1686–1724) built a full-sized flying-machine which remained earthbound, in spite of its title of the 'Passarola' or 'Great Bird'. In appearance resembling a Viking longship with wings and a bird tail, the Passarola had its lift augmented by a large horizontal sail or canopy. A model built in 1709 is supposed to have made a short gliding flight. Others to follow the Gusmão line of thought included the Swede, Emmanuel Swedenborg, who in 1716 began to write his book, *Daedalus Hyperboreas,* containing details of a flying-machine with a car slung under a canopy, which could be reefed like a sail, propulsion being supplied by spring-powered flappers. Then in 1772, Canon Desforges, of Etampes, built and attempted to fly, from a tower, a *'voiture volante'*, consisting of a wickerwork basket with a canopy to provide lift, and flappers for propulsion. Jean Pierre Blanchard, who was later to gain fame and distinction as a balloonist, produced a design for a canopied and flapper-powered flying-machine in 1781, but when built, this proved to be as hopeless as the rest of its kind.

The Desforges example shows that tower jumping was not dead at such a late stage, even though discredited by the revelations of Borelli, Hooke and Willughby. Indeed, thirty years earlier, in 1742, the Marquis de Bacqueville had jumped from a riverside house in Paris and, with wings attached to arms and legs, had attempted to fly across the River Seine, falling into a barge and breaking both legs in the attempt, which was a complete failure.

During the mid-eighteenth century, which must also be considered as the final years of earthbound activity, evidence of a more scientific approach may be detected. Then, too, post-Rennaissance and Reformation Europe possessed many philosophers and scientists outside the Church, which in more troubled times had tended to act as a refuge for such people.

The Russians credit Michael Vasilyevitch Lomonosov with building a clockwork-powered twin contra-rotating rotor, helicopter model in 1754, which they claim was capable of flight. But there is no evidence to support this and, bearing in mind the excessive claim for Mozhaiski from Russia, the authenticity of the claim must be doubted strongly.

Melchior Bauer in 1764 designed a fixed-wing flying-machine, which was man-powered using a system of rockering flap-valves, while in 1781, Karl Friedrich Meerwein built a glider with ornithopter assistance, which made a short glide. Before this, A. J. P. Paucton, a French mathematician, proposed in his *Theorie de la Vis Archimede*, a man-powered helicopter which would obtain lift from one airscrew, and propulsion from another.

The first recorded scientific use of the kite came in 1749, when the then Professor of Astronomy at Glasgow University, Alexander Wilson, was able to record the temperature of clouds at 3,000 feet using a thermometer attached to a train of four kites. He is also believed to have studied atmospheric electricity using kites, although history credits this achievement first to the American, Benjamin Franklin, in 1752 while flying a kite in a thunderstorm.

Air-mindedness was growing at this point, and the signs of this were both in the increasing activity by the experimenters and the greater incidences of references to flight or to space travel in the literature of the period. Amongst those who thought flight worthy of at least a mention could be included Joseph Addison, Jonathan Swift in *Gulliver's Travels* (1726), Doctor Samuel Johnson in 'The Rambler' (1752), and La Follie, as well as many less famous literary figures. A sign of change, no doubt, but in the years to come truth would be stranger than any fiction, for in 1776, Henry Cavendish had succeeded in isolating hydrogen, while, still in England, Joseph Black had suggested experiments with hydrogen-filled soap bubbles to show the lifting power of the new element and Tiberius Cavallo carried out these experiments.

1 'The Flight of Daedalus and Fall of Icarus', a woodcut from Riederer's *Spiegel der Wahren Rhetoric*, published in 1493 and the first known printed representation of flight. Undoubtedly the most famous of the many legends concerning flight, that of Daedalus and his son Icarus has inspired a number of artists as well as more than a few tower jumpers. (Photo: Science Museum, London).

2 King Kai Kawus of Persia in his chariot drawn by eagles. This illustration from an Ancient Persian manuscript is based upon a legend of about 1500 BC, and the Macedonian, Alexander the Great, is accorded a similar experience. (Photo: Science Museum, London).

3 Roger Bacon (c. 1214–94), the Franciscan monk who was also the first writer on the possibilities of flight. (Photo: Science Museum, London).

6 A self-portrait of the Italian artist, Leonardo da Vinci, who produced the first considered designs for flying-machines, as well as for a number of items of what might today be described as ancillary equipment. His approach, though brilliant, might best be considered as romantic rather than scientific. (Photo: Science Museum, London).

4 One of the earliest illustrations of a European plane-surface kite, published in 1634 in Bate's *Mysteryes of Nature and Art*. Many kites of the period were in fact dragon-shaped, this no doubt having some connection with their country of origin. (Photo: Science Museum, London).

5 The design for an aerial ship, supported aloft by four copper spheres empty of air, and published in 1670 by a Jesuit priest, Father Francesco de Lana de Terzi. This design can be considered to be prophetic in a number of aspects. (Photo: Science Museum, London).

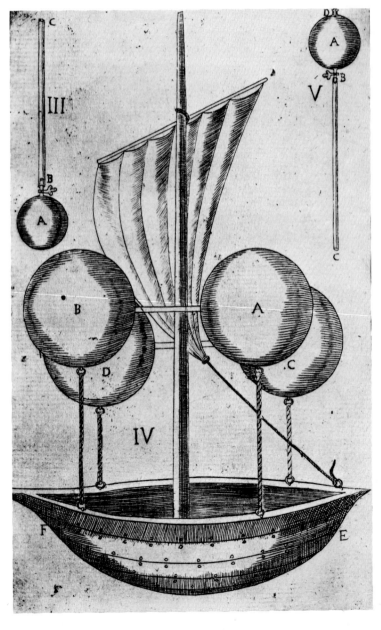

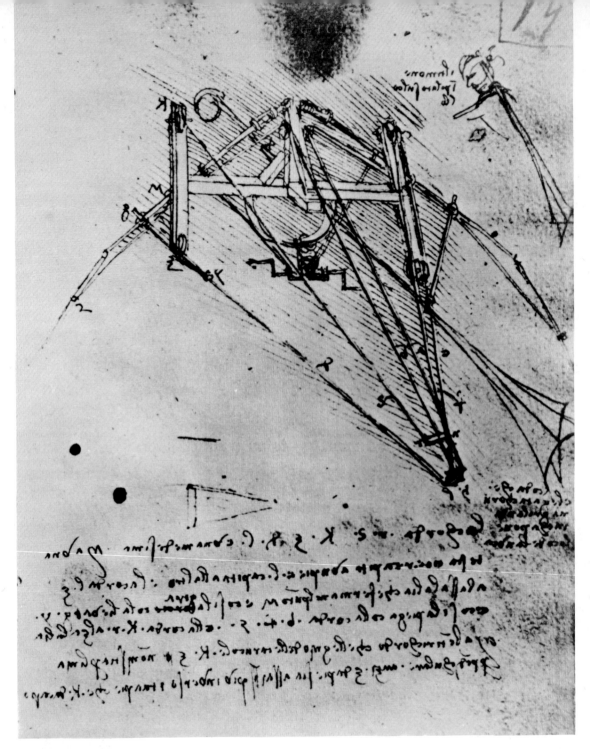

7 The Da Vinci design for a prone-type ornithopter with rudder control. A characteristic of many of his designs was the dependence on what might almost be described as a 'rowing' action for flight. (Photo: Science Museum, London).

8 A spring-operated ornithopter, also by Leonardo da Vinci. (Photo: Science Museum, London)

▶

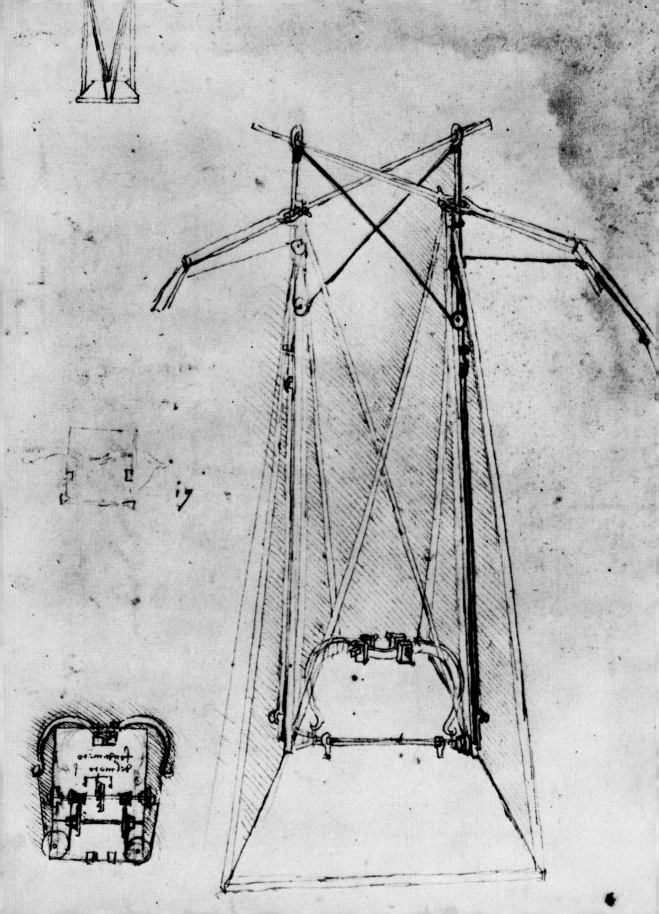

9 One of the more realistic Da Vinci designs, this vague sketch shows a rudimentary hang-glider, was produced during the latter part of his life, and seems to have been an isolated instance of interest in fixed-wing glider design. (Photo: Science Museum, London).

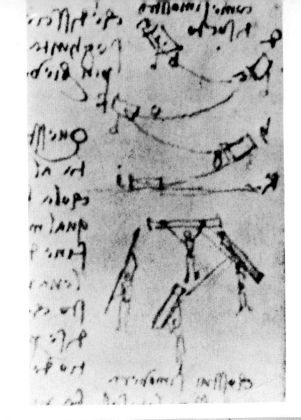

10 Although bearing some resemblance to the hang-glider designs of four hundred years later, this particular Da Vinci design was in fact for a fixed-wing aircraft with the outer wing hinged for flapper propulsion. Generally, this design is accepted as having limited possibilities for flight under modern conditions. (Photo: Science Museum, London).

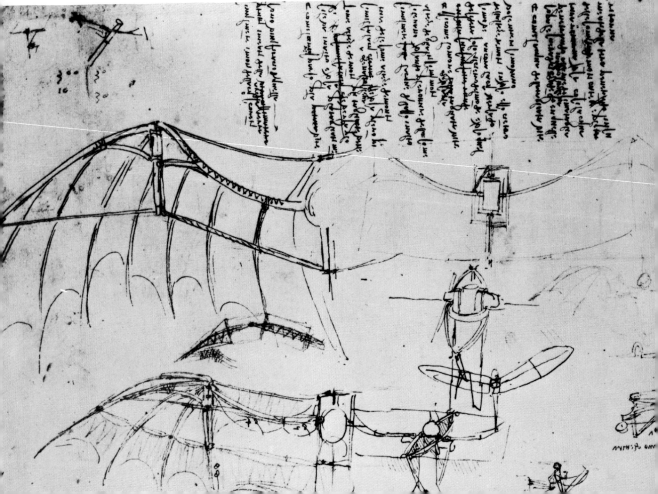

11 A model of Da Vinci's helicopter design, consisting of a helical screw which would have been powered by a clockwork motor. This design probably originated during the middle years of the artist's life, around 1500. (Crown Copyright, Science, Museum, London).

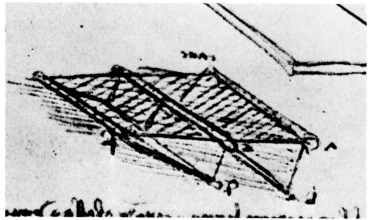

12 Leonardo da Vinci's sketched design for a flap valve, intended to assist ornithopter control. (Photo: Science Museum, London).

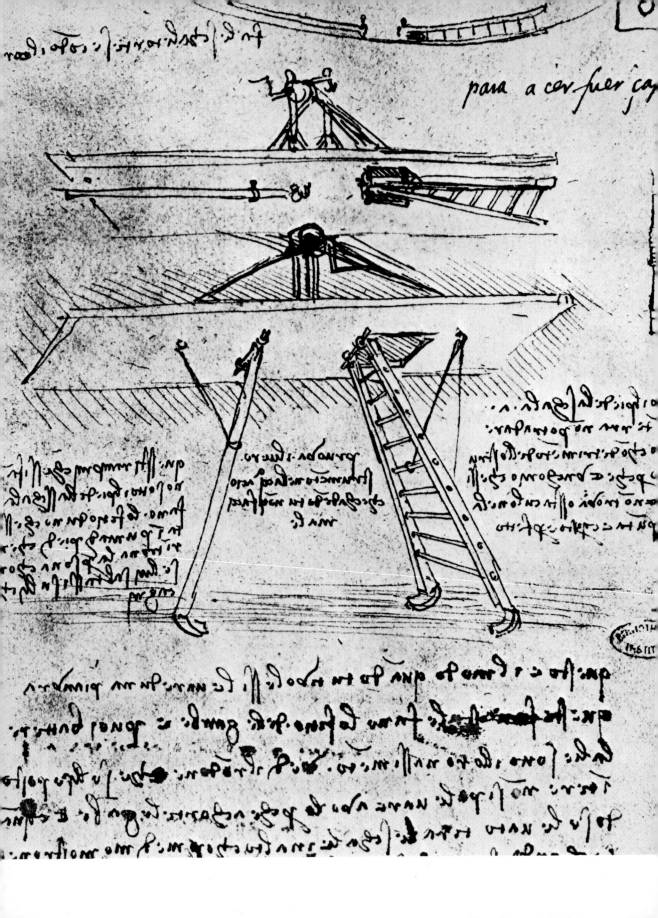

13 Perhaps the most remarkable glimpse into the future by Da Vinci was this design for a retractable undercarriage, although certainly of novel layout! The lower part of the design shows the undercarriage in the 'down' position, while above there is an impression of the 'retracted' position. It can only be surmised that the idea of a retractable undercarriage in Da Vinci's time owed more to either an interest in gadgetry or to neatness than to any aerodynamic considerations. (Photo: Science Museum, London).

◀

14 A model reproduction of Da Vinci's parachute design, originally produced in 1485 and the oldest known design for a parachute. Obviously, such a device would be clumsy and useless for escape purposes, depending as it does on so much fixed structure, and it must be regarded as yet another design for the tower jumper. (Crown Copyright, Science Museum, London).

15 The first published design for a parachute, by the Italian Fausto Veranzio in 1595 and based on a ship's sail. This illustration was included in Veranzio's work, *Machinae Novae*. (Photo: Science Museum, London).

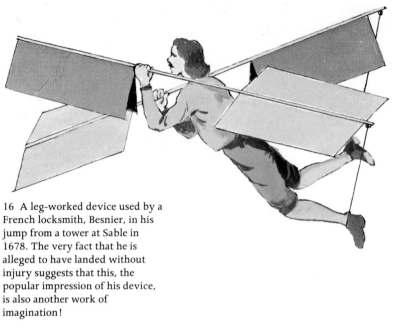

16 A leg-worked device used by a French locksmith, Besnier, in his jump from a tower at Sable in 1678. The very fact that he is alleged to have landed without injury suggests that this, the popular impression of his device, is also another work of imagination!

17 The 'Passarola', or 'Great Bird' of the Brazilian priest, Gusmão, which is supposed to have been built during the early years of the eighteenth century. If it was built, it can be counted as the first full-sized flying machine, but evidence is scant and no claim seems to have been made for flight for the full-sized version, although a model is claimed to have made a short gliding flight.

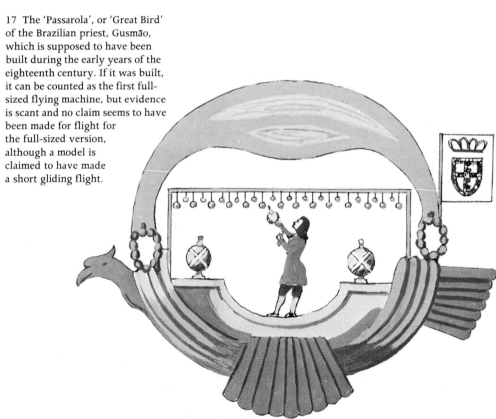

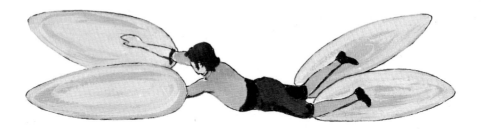

18 The attempt by the Marquis de Bacqueville to fly across the Seine in 1742. It is probable that the wings were in fact larger than those shown, but even so, the fact that he broke both legs in the attempt is hardly surprising.

Chapter 2

UP, UP AND AWAY

Early balloon ascents, the Montgolfier brothers, pioneering
flights, military applications, showmanship, parachute jumps,
Charles, Garnerin, artillery rockets.

*'I have not the smallest molecule of faith
in aerial navigation other than
ballooning.'*

LORD KELVIN, 1896

Success has a habit of coming suddenly and often in the least expected manner. It is a matter for debate whether mankind inches forward or whether vast strides are made, interspersed with long periods of stagnation, but in any account of the early days of flight, it would certainly seem that within a few short months mankind ceased to be earthbound and took to the skies after more than two thousand years spent in fruitless attempts to become airborne. Viewed in retrospect, De Lana's design for an aerial ship had an air of the prophetic about it, while other apparently more exciting designs could only suggest hopelessness.

The brothers, Joseph Michel (1740–1810) and Jacques Étienne (1745–99) Montgolfier, two paper-makers from Annonay, near Lyons, had noticed ash and unburnt particles rising in the smoke and heat of a fire. After placing paper bags in the smoke, probably in late 1782, and watching these rise, they made a large paper and linen sphere, which was placed over a fire of chopped wool and straw in the market place at Annonay, from which it made an ascent on 4th June, 1783, before a large and admiring crowd. Journeying to Paris later during that eventful summer, they constructed a larger balloon, which made an ascent on 19th September from the Palace of Versailles, carrying a cock, a sheep and a duck on an eight minute, two mile voyage, eventually ending with a safe landing in the Bois de Vaucressan. This, the first aerial voyage in history, was watched by Louis XVI of France, his wife, Marie Antionette, and a crowd reputed to have been around 130,000 strong.

Before this, however, the news of the successful ascent of the Montgolfière balloon, as the hot-air balloon became known, in the market place at Annonay had already reached the Académie des Sciences in Paris. It was immediately assumed that the brothers had discovered a new gas, and indeed the Montgolfier brothers themselves were of this opinion, but they knew that the gas was a good deal heavier than hydrogen, discovered by Cavendish in 1776, and of which a great deal had become known through the work of Black and Cavallo.

The eminent professor, Jacques Alexander César Charles (1746–1823), was commissioned to build a suitable rival to the Montgolfière, using hydrogen, which he was able to do with the aid of the Roberts brothers, who had developed a new rubberised silk fabric. The problem of producing a sufficient quantity of hydrogen, then no mean task, was solved by the action of sulphuric acid on scrap iron. A small hydrogen balloon was launched from the Champ de Mars on 27th August, 1783, before a large crowd, which included the illustrious American scientist, Benjamin Franklin. It travelled for forty-five minutes and fifteen miles to the village of Genoesse, where it was attacked by frightened peasants on landing.

The first manned ascent in a balloon was by François Pilâtre de Rozier (1757–85), who made an ascent in a tethered Montgolfière on 15th October, 1783. It was intended that two convicts should make the first aerial voyage by men, rather as the discoverers of America had frequently to resort to the jails for their crews, but Pilâtre de Rozier and the Marquis d'Arlandes volunteered, becoming the first men to fulfil the age-old dream of voyaging through the skies on 21st November, 1783. The two men ascended from the gardens of the Chateau la Muette in the Bois de Boulogne, near Paris, and then travelled over the city before descending on the Butte-aux-Cailles, some five-and-a-half miles from their starting point. Unlike the farm animals which had 'volunteered' for the September flight, D'Arlandes and Pilâtre de Rozier had sponges and buckets of water to control their straw and wool fire – a mixture of combustibles which the Montgolfiers credited with considerable properties.

Only ten days separated the first and second aerial voyages by men in history, with the first manned ascent by a Charlière, or hydrogen balloon, taking place on 1st December, 1783. On that date, Jacques Charles and one of his associates, Aîné Robert, ascended from the Tuileries Gardens in Paris, watched by a crowd recorded as numbering some 400,000 – an incredible figure! Charles and Robert journeyed twenty-seven miles before landing at the small town of Nesles, although Aîné Robert then left the balloon and the ballast was jettisoned, allowing Charles to travel a further four-and-a-half miles in the much-lightened balloon. The Charlière balloon rather than the Montgolfière set the pattern for subsequent development of the concept, possessing a true spherical shape, with a valve in the crown for venting gas, a net slung over the envelope from which the car or gondolier was slung, equipped with ballast, and using a simple barometer altimeter – possibly the only significant difference from hydrogen balloons of a very much later period was the absence of a ripping panel.

Joseph Montgolfier's contribution to flight did not end with a simple balloon ascent. In a paper delivered to the University of Lyons in October, 1783, he told of experiments with reaction propulsion, described as requiring openings in the side of the balloon opposite to the direction in which travel was desired. The experiments failed, in spite of the soundness of the theory, because the vehicle, a Montgolfière, did not possess the necessary pressure in the envelope for a substantial thrust.

Heavier-than-air flight was not neglected during this time of success for lighter-than-air flight. In 1784, in Paris, Launoy and Bienvenu produced a working model of a helicopter, with a two-bladed rotor on each end of a pole and worked by a bow-drill mechanism which was wound, the propellers turning in opposite directions or contra-rotating. Although less exciting than the exploits of the balloonists, and probably fairly unspectacular, the Launoy and Bienvenu experiment led directly to all subsequent successful helicopter experiments. Then another Frenchman, A. J. Renaux, produced an ornithopter design, without ever actually building even a model, and Gérard also designed an ornithopter, but had the realism to suggest that some form of mechanical propulsion be used. Not withstanding all that had passed before, one, Aries, made what can best be described as a tower jump at Embrun, although he used wings and managed sufficient 'glide' effect to avoid serious injury. An engraving of the period showed 'balloon jumpers', but there is no documentation to indicate that this was anything other than an imaginative play on the tower jumping theme. In many ways, 1784 had been eventful enough as it was without such innovations.

Women got into the air with balloons rather sooner after the first ascent than after the first aeroplane flight or the first manned space-flight, which is either a reflection on the barriers which may have been actually created, rather than removed, by emancipation, or an indication of the rapid acceptance of the balloon by late eighteenth century society. Shortly after the first manned aerial voyages, exhibition ascents were given by the Montgolfier brothers, and on 20th May, 1784, no less than four women, the Marchioness de Montalembert, the Countess de Montalembert, the Countess de Podenas and Mademoiselle de Lagarde, rose from the Faubourg St. Antoine in Paris in a tethered balloon. The first aerial voyage by a woman occurred on 4th June, 1784, when a Madame Thible made an ascent in a Montgolfière at Lyons, with a Monsieur Fleurant for company and an audience which included the King of Sweden.

Not all of the excitement was confined to France. On 25th February, 1784, a Montgolfière had made an ascent at Moncuco, near Milan, carrying Chevalier Paul Andreani with Augusta and Charles Gerli. A fairly mundane ascent, rising to only five hundred feet or so, was made in Scotland on 25th August by James Tytler, rising from the Heriot's Garden in Edinburgh. It fell to an Italian diplomat, Vincenzo Lunardi, to make the first hydrogen balloon ascent in the United Kingdom when, on 15th September, 1784, he travelled in a Charlière from the Honourable Artillery Company's parade ground at Moorfields in the City of London to North Mimms in Hertfordshire, where he jettisoned his ballast and his only passenger, a pet cat, in order to continue his voyage, eventually descending at Standon Green End, near Ware, also in Hertfordshire. In June, 1785, Lunardi arranged the first flight by a woman in the British Isles, with Mrs. Letitia Ann Sage due to travel with Lunardi, a Mr George Biggin and a Colonel Hastings from St George's Fields, London, on the 29th. Mrs Sage was grossly overweight, and in order that the flight could take place, Lunardi and Hastings had to forego their places on the flight, which eventually ended at Harrow, in Middlesex.

Attempts to try and exercise some control over the balloon were not long in coming. One of the first was by a Father Miolan and a Monsieur Juninet, who attempted to use the Montgolfier system of reaction propulsion in a large Montgolfière balloon, but this failed to rise from the ground, let alone propel itself, on 11th July, 1784, at the Luxembourg Gardens in Paris. It is recorded that a disappointed and angry crowd destroyed the balloon, which eventually caught fire. Another attempt at propulsion and control of balloons came from Jean Pierre Blanchard, who fitted a six-bladed airscrew or 'moulinet' to a Charlière balloon, in which he made an ascent over London on 16th October, 1784, rising from Chelsea with Dr John Sheldon of the Royal Academy; the hand-operated airscrew proved to be completely ineffectual.

Blanchard was nevertheless soon to earn himself a more positive place in the history of flight than either his 1781 design for a flying-machine or his tentative attempts at balloon propulsion could merit. On the 7th January, 1785, accompanied by an American, Dr John Jeffries, Blanchard made an ascent from Dover Castle at 1 pm and landed safely in the Bois de Felmores, in France, two-and-a-half hours later after an eventful flight in a Charlière balloon, in which they jettisoned not only their ballast, but part of their clothing as well. According to the account by a contemporary chronicler – none other than Tiberius Cavallo – the day was warm after a very frosty night, and the balloon had difficulty in rising off the ground at Dover. Most of the ballast had to be jettisoned in order to start the voyage, and books and parts of the gondolier, with food and drink, had to be thrown away during the voyage across the English Channel.

Always something of a showman, Blanchard toured Europe making exhibition ascents, usually entertaining large crowds for which he introduced the added, and one would have thought unnecessary, attraction of sending down small animals from his balloon by parachute. He could hardly claim a scientific interest in such action since he is not known to have made any parachute descents himself. His sole remaining distinction after the cross-Channel flight was to make the first balloon ascent in the United States, travelling from Philadelphia to Gloucester County, New Jersey, on 9th January, 1793. Most of his balloons had airscrews or flappers, and sometimes steering oars – all of which were useless. He died in 1809 at the age of fifty-six. Ten years after his death, his widow, who also made exhibition ascents with the then not un-usual feature of dropping fireworks by parachute from the balloon, was killed in an accident at the Tivoli Gardens in Paris. The cause of the accident was the fire carried to light the fireworks, which set fire to the hydrogen balloon, resulting in a rapid loss of height and Madame Blanchard fell to her death from the roof of a house onto which the balloon had descended.

A rather more practical approach to the propulsion of lighter-than-air vehicles than that of Blanchard had appeared in 1785, with the publication by Lieutenant (later General) Jean Baptiste Marie Meusnier (1754–93) of his plans for a dirigible balloon, to be propelled by three airscrews. Unfortunately, this design was never built.

Less happily, the first attempt at a France to England crossing of the Channel ended in tragedy, with the first fatal ballooning accident at Huitmile Warren, near Boulogne on the French coast, on 15th June, 1785. The victims were François Pilâtre de Rozier and a companion, Jules Romain, who had just risen from Boulogne in a balloon using the almost unbelievably dangerous combination of hydrogen and a Montgolfière-style fire in a brazier to keep the hydrogen expanded and minimise the chances of a repeat of Blanchard's problems. Either the fire set the balloon alight, or there was a leak of hydrogen with the same end result.

A practical use for the balloon was soon discovered. It was during the Napoleonic wars that the French republican forces discovered the potential of the captive balloon for air observation and artillery spotting duties – the object of having the balloon tethered being to prevent its falling into enemy hands and to reduce any delay in obtaining information from the observers. The first recorded use of a balloon for artillery spotting was at the Battle of Maubeuge in 1794, when a captive hydrogen balloon, *L'Entreprenent*, was supposed to have played a decisive part in the battle. The balloon later appeared at the Siege of Charleroi and at the Battle of Fleurus, on 26th June, 1794, and also at other battles, including Mayence on the River Rhine. Capitaine Jean Marie Joseph Coutelle (1748–1835) was made '*chef du bataillon de aérostiers de la République*, or the first squadron leader in fact.

Balloons, and in particular the Montgolfière type, were in effect their own parachute, since even a leak in a hydrogen balloon did not automatically entail an over-rapid descent, unless fire occurred. The Montgolfière variety may not have been particularly efficient, suffering from heat loss by the very nature of their design, but they could also make a tolerable parachute.

At about the time of the first balloon ascents, however, another Frenchman, Sebastien Lenormand, made a descent from an observation tower at Montpellier using a form of parachute with a braced canopy. It remained for yet another Frenchman, André Joseph Garnerin (1770–1825), to make the first real parachute descent in history, on 22nd October, 1797. Garnerin first rose in a hydrogen balloon with the parachute closed, then releasing the balloon and descending in the car or gondolier under the parachute, which opened out successfully. The large ribbed parasol of the Garnerin parachute did not differ too greatly from the parachute of today, except that there were no vents, that any control of the direction of the descent was impossible, and the car and its occupant were subjected to considerable swaying during the descent.

Garnerin, apart from possessing considerable courage, had the flair for showmanship which characterised so many of the early aeronauts. He made numerous parachute descents, always detaching a hydrogen balloon leaving the car to descend under a parachute. His imitators were many, because a balloon ascent with a parachute descent proved to be rather more of an attraction at a fairground or festival than a straightforward balloon ascent, and this was certainly saying something. Most often, hot-air balloons were used by the parachutists, since apart from the lower initial cost, these were also easily recovered after the air had cooled and the balloon descended.

Although, by the early years of the nineteenth century, the balloon had become an accepted fact, and almost a workaday tool in some limited respects, the lack of any real competition from other forms of flight, and the time taken to develop a practical dirigible, meant that the balloon did not lose its novelty value during the century and more which followed. Always a crowd-puller, and even more so if a parachute descent could be added, the balloon became very much a showman's gimmick, usually with the cheaper hot-air balloon being used, or coal gas being substituted for costly hydrogen if the more expensive Charlière type was considered worthwhile. Comparisons between the early days of ballooning and the early days of spaceflight cannot easily be made.

A final point of interest, spanning the closing years of the eighteenth and the early years of the nineteenth century, although of little immediate importance to man's early years in the air, was the re-invention of the artillery rocket in Europe by Sir William Congreve. At that time, the artillery rocket was a relatively new arrival from China in India, where it was used by the Tipu Sultan's troops against the Duke of Wellington's army in 1799. News of the battle, and of the use of war or artillery rockets, eventually reached England, and undoubtedly inspired Congreve, who conducted the first trial firings of the 'new' weapon in 1805. By 1807, the Royal Navy had sufficient confidence in the new weapon to use it in a bombardment of Copenhagen, with some considerable effect. The development owes more to the history of artillery than to the history of flight, since rocket-powered manned flight did not become possible until well after the end of World War I, although the possibilities for the future must be regarded as considerable.

LES FRÈRES MONTGOLFIER.

1 The Montgolfier brothers, Joseph Michel and
Jacques Étienne, respectively aged 43 years and
38 years at the time of their first balloon ascents
from Paris. Papermakers by trade, their interest
in the possibilities of flight came almost by
accident, since there is no evidence of any life-
long search for means of flight by either
brother, although Joseph did undertake some
experiments into the possibilities of propulsion.
(Photo: Library of Congress, Washington)

Plate I.

AERONAUTICS.

Montgolfiers Balloon

Blanchards Balloon

Lanas Aeronautic Machine

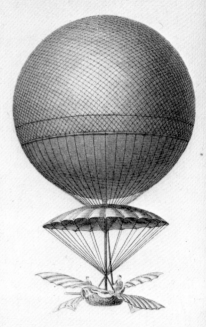

Garnerin Ascending

Charles & Roberts' Balloon

Garnerin Descending

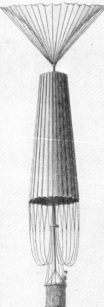

form of the Wings employed by Lunardi

Fig. 7

form of the Wings employed by Blanchard

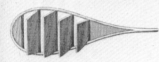

Drawn by Joseph Clement.

Published as the Act directs April 1818, by Rest Fenner, Paternoster Row.

Engraved by A.W. Warren & J. Davis

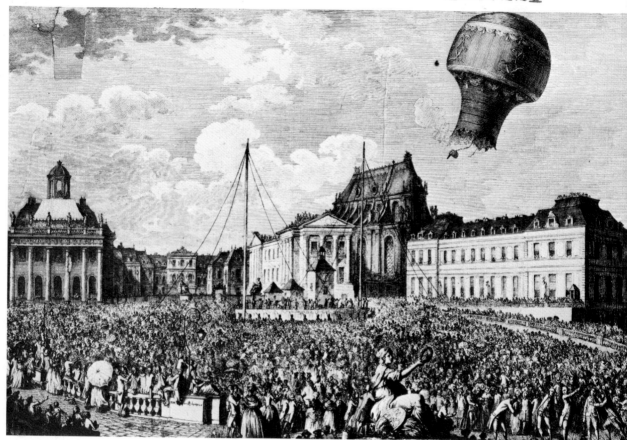

3 *'Experience Aerostatique'* is the original sub-title to this
illustration, with which one must imagine the vast crowd of
spectators to be in agreement! In fact 130,000 people were
supposed to have watched the first aerial voyage, which took
a cock, a sheep and a duck from Versailles under a bright blue
and gold Montgolfier hot air balloon on 19th September, 1783.
Distinguished spectators included Louis XVI of France, and
his wife, Marie 'let them eat cake' Antionette.
(Photo: Science Museum, London).

2 The Montgolfière balloon and others, an early attempt at
showing progress in aerostation and dating from 1818.
(Photo: Library of Congress, Washington).

4 Before committing themselves to
a voyage in a Montgolfière, the
intrepid balloonists conducted
trials with a tethered, or captive,
balloon in Paris on 15th October,
1783. One of the occupants of the
balloon on this occasion was
François Pilâtre de Rozier.
Maximum height gained on this
occasion is supposed to have been
about 84 feet, with the balloon
straining at the retaining ropes.
(Photo: Science Museum, London).

5 François Pilâtre de Rozier (1757–85), whose distinguished career as a balloonist included the first manned balloon ascent and the first manned aerial voyage, before becoming one of the first two men to be killed in a ballooning accident. (Photo: Library of Congress, Washington).

6 The dreams of centuries came true on 21st November, 1783, with the first aerial voyage by man. François Pilâtre de Rozier and the Marquis d'Arlandes are seen here ascending from the grounds of the Chateau la Muette, which also happened to be the site of the earlier tethered trials.
(Photo: Science Museum, London).

7 Jacques Alexander César
Charles, was astronomy professor
at the Académie des Sciences in
Paris at the time of the
Montgolfier experiments. He was
able to design and build the first
hydrogen balloons in a very short
time. In this illustration, he is seen
shortly before making the first
balloon ascent. (Photo: Library
of Congress, Washington).

8 Alarm at Genoesse! Before venturing on an aerial
voyage, Charles and his much under-valued partners, the
Roberts brothers, dispatched a smaller unmanned
hydrogen balloon from Paris on 27th August, 1783,
which landed at the village of Genoesse, only to be
attacked by a crowd of terrified peasants who thought
that it had come from the Devil. (Photo: Library of
Congress, Washington).

Allarme Générale des Habitants de Gonesse, occasionée par la chute du Ballon Aréostatique de M. De Monge...

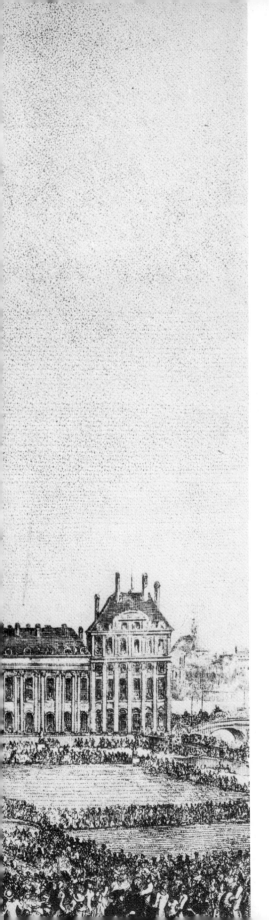

9 The second manned aerial voyage, and the first by a hydrogen balloon, rising from the Tuileries Gardens in Paris on 1st December, 1783, with J.A.C. Charles and Ainé Robert. Although most accounts claim that the crowd of onlookers numbered 400,000, the original caption to this illustration suggests twice that figure. The balloon is also stated to be red and white – in fact some of the accounts of the early balloon ascents would do justice to a mannequin parade! (Photo: Science Museum, London).

10 A diorama of the Charlière ascent of 1st December, 1783, showing in the foreground the apparatus used at the time for filling the balloon envelope. (Crown Copyright, Science Museum, London).

11 Souvenirs! Indeed, the late eighteenth and the nineteenth century showed a degree of ingenuity in this particular business activity which seems to have been lost since, in spite of the opportunities afforded by the tourist industry and modern scientific achievements. This elaborate handkerchief portrays the Charlière as a centrepiece, with reproductions of the apparatus for filling the balloon envelope on each of the sides, and representations of Charles, one of the Robert brothers and one of the Montgolfier brothers, with Louis XIV, in the corners. (Crown Copyright, Science Museum, London).

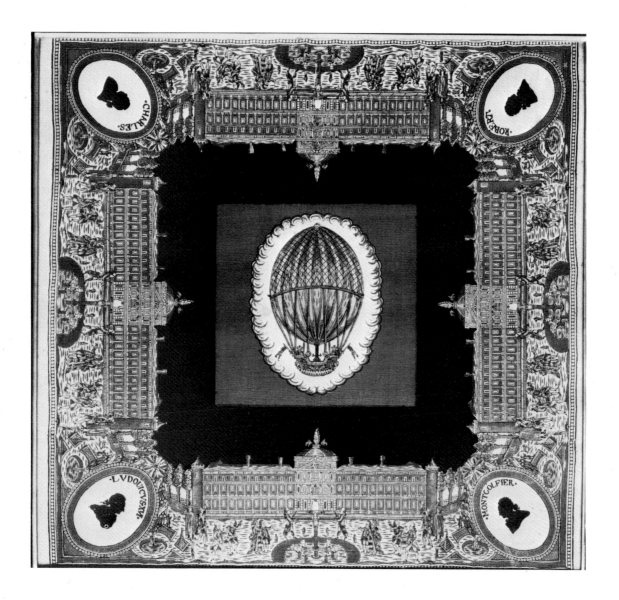

Mgr. le Duc de Chartres et M.^{r.} le Duc de Fitz Jame
signent le Procès Verbal qui constate l'arrivée de MM. Charles et Robert
dans la Prairie de Nesle près d'Hedouville.
A Paris chez Tilliard Graveur, Quai des Grands Augustins,
Maison de M.I. Debure Fils Ainé, Libraire.

12 'Le retour du Globe Aerostatique' to Paris on Tuesday, 2nd December, 1783. Obviously much deflated, we are not told whether this was due to natural leakage or to intentional venting in order to fit the balloon on to the horse-drawn wagon. The crowd, also much reduced, seems to have been excited, nevertheless. (Photo: Bibliothèque Nationale, Paris).

13 'Troisième Voyage Aérien'. An ascent by the Montgolfière, 'Le Flesselle', on 19th January, 1784, at Lyons. This was the first of a number of demonstration ascents at Lyons and Paris. It can be guessed that 'Le Flesselle' was, from the illustration, a larger balloon than any built previously by the brothers, and this is borne out by a contemporary account. Apparently, Joseph Montgolfier and Pilâtre de Rozier intended to take four noblemen with them on the ascent, but became concerned about the ability of the balloon to lift such a load. The noblemen insisted on remaining on the balloon to the point of drawing their swords, but Montgolfier and Pilâtre de Rozier managed to get aboard at the last moment, as did a young stowaway, and the balloon did manage to lift its load. (Photo: Science Museum, London).

14 Landing formalities, 1783! Really, not a case of the bureaucracy being quick off the mark, but instead a simple declaration by the Duke of Chartres and the Duke of Fitz Jame affirming the Charlière's landing on the Plain of Nesle on 1st December, 1783. The balloon had been followed on horseback from Paris by the two aristocrats and a number of other distinguished persons. Robert left the balloon at this point, and thus lightened it was able to carry Charles further. (Photo: Science Museum, London).

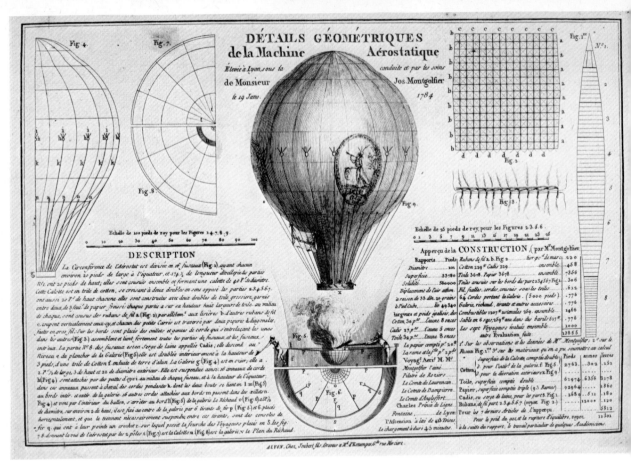

Detailed engraving titled "DÉTAILS GÉOMÉTRIQUES de la Machine Aérostatique"

15 A detail of the Montgolfière, 'Le Flesselle', although it could be any balloon of this type given due allowance for changes in measurements. (Photo: Science Museum, London).

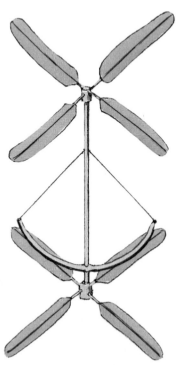

16 The Launoy and Bienvenu helicopter model of 1784, which can be accepted as the forerunner of all subsequent successful helicopter development, as well as designs for simple toys.

46

The **ENGLISH BALLOON** and Appendages *in which Mr LUNARDI ascended into the Atmosphere from the Artillery Ground, Sep.r 15 1784.*

17 The first hydrogen balloon ascent in the United Kingdom was left to an Italian diplomat, Vincenzo Lunardi, from Tuscany, who rose from the Honourable Artillery Company's parade ground in the City of London. This took place on 15th September, 1784. This illustration is a detail of his balloon, although others show four flapper blades instead of the two shown here. A small crowd of spectators seems to have been present at the time, although they are not shown in this illustration. (Photo: Science Museum, London).

18 Simply the apparatus for filling Mr Lunardi's balloon! The manufacture of hydrogen at this time was a complicated and messy business, and no doubt the resultant gas was far from pure and the danger of leakage while filling the balloon's envelope very real. (Photo: Science Museum, London).

19 Jean Pierre Blanchard, one of the most famous of the early balloonists. An exhibitionist, even by the standards of the aeronauts of the day, he was also a generally unsuccessful experimenter who seems to have grasped little about the facts of aeronautics. He eventually died from a heart attack while ballooning. (Photo: Library of Congress, Washington).

20 Claimed by the artist to be an exact representation of the departure of Blanchard and his American companion, Dr Jeffries, from Dover Castle on 7th January, 1785, and the low height of the balloon lends credibility to this claim since the entire flight across the English Channel was in constant danger of ditching in the sea. It might have been more interesting to see the state of the balloon and its passengers at the end of the journey, after they had jettisoned everything possible! The implication of some accounts of the flight seems to be that the balloon was really overloaded, which could have been the sole cause of the problems experienced in attempting to stay aloft. Note the flappers, a device in which Blanchard never lost faith. (Photo: Science Museum, London).

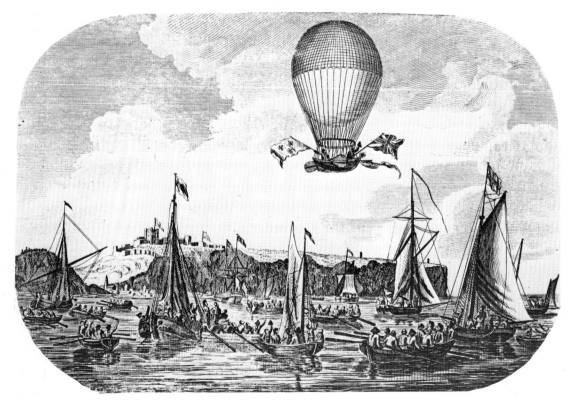

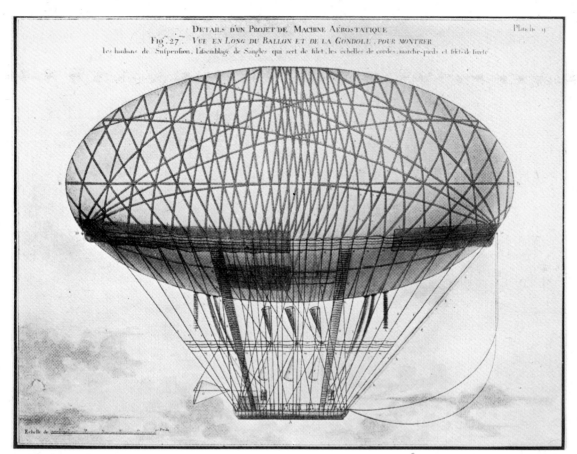

21 The first airship design in the accepted sense of the term, by General Jean Baptiste Marie Meusner in 1784. This '*Project de Machine Aérostatique*' was never built, probably due in no small part to problems of construction and of producing sufficient gas to fill the vast envelope. Even if built, there would have remained the problem of finding a suitable powerplant. (Photo: Science Museum, London).

22 The death of Pilâtre de Rozier and his companion, Jules Romain, shortly after the start of their attempt to cross the English Channel from France to England on 15th June, 1785. The accident, caused by the dangerous combination of a hydrogen balloon with a Montgolfier-style brazier slung underneath to heat the gas, fired the public imagination and was featured on a number of souvenirs, including snuff boxes! This was the first ballooning accident.

23 The first aerial voyage by an English woman, Mrs Letitia Ann Sage, seen here rising in Vincenzo Lunardi's 'new' balloon from St George's Fields, near London, on 29th June, 1785. Her companion is George Biggin. The flight ended at Harrow with a confrontation with an irate farmer. This is probably the most accurate of the several illustrations which exist to record this event. (Photo: Science Museum, London).

The THREE FAVORITE AERIAL TRAVELLERS.
Vincent Lunardi Esq. first *Aeronaut in England.*
George Biggin Esq.
and *M.rs Sage first English Female Aerial Traveller.*

24 A detail showing Mrs Sage and her companions, Vincenzo Lunardi and, waving his hat, George Biggin. Leaving aside the differences in the gondola, the illustration is also at variance with the generally accepted story that Lunardi and a Colonel Hastings stood down from the flight rather than draw attention to Mrs Sage's weight of more than 200 lbs! The artist would seem to have been at pains to flatter Mrs Sage. (Photo: Bibliothèque Nationale, Paris).

50

25 Balloons at war! This illustration
of a captive balloon in use at the
Battle of Fleurus in 1794 is taken
from the lid of a snuff box. (Crown
Copyright, Science Museum,
London).

26 Balloons at war again. Fortunately, this idea did not progress beyond this threatening illustration of giant Montgolfière balloons, capable of carrying 3,000 men each, for an invasion of England. Cavalry and artillery seem to have been intended for such an expedition as well, while large lamps would have kept Napoleon's army above Britannia's rule of the waves! (Photo: Science Museum, London).

27 A parachute jump by André Garnerin on 21st September, 1802, near St Pancras, London. This was probably one of his first descents in England and, although coming some five years after his original descent, seems to have been the cause of considerable public excitement and commotion, to which a wheelbarrow-load of fruit has fallen victim. It can clearly be seen that Garnerin descended in the gondola of the balloon, and the artist has managed to convey the swaying motion to which the Garnerin parachute was subject. (Photo: Science Museum, London).

▼

28 'Project d'une Nouvelle Messagerie', which, with the similar 'Aérostat de Poste', which differed only in minor details, must rank high amongst any list of incredible illustrations for futuristic balloon projects. Intended to carry some 20,000 passengers for China and to depa on 10th May, 2440, taking about 32 days for the round-trip voyag the project can be dismissed as p fantasy and lacks any prophetic features. (Photo: Bibliothèque Nationale, Paris).

▶

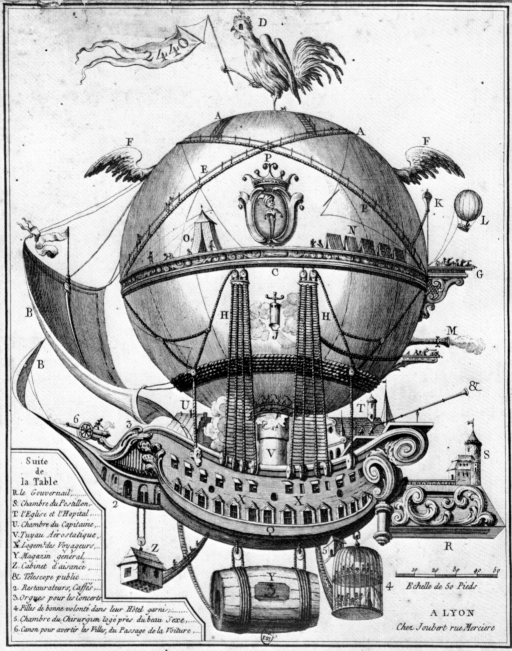

2440

Suite
de
la Table

R. le Gouvernail.............
S. Chambre du Postillon.
T. l'Eglise et l'Hôpital..
U. Chambre du Capitaine..
V. Tuyau Aérostatique.....
X. Logemens des Voyageurs....
Y. Magazin général.......
Z. Cabinet d'aisance........
&. Télescope public...........
2. Restaurateurs, Caffés....
3. Orgues pour les Concerts.
4. Filles de bonne volonté dans leur Hôtel garni.
5. Chambre du Chirurgien logé près du beau Sexe.
6. Canon pour avertir les Villes, du Passage de la Voiture.

Echelle de 50 Pieds

10   20   30   40   50

A LYON
Chez Joubert rue Mercière.

PROJET D'UNE NOUVELLE MESSAGERIE.

Les Entrepreneurs jaloux d'acquérir à leur voiture une préférence marquée sur toutes celles en usage jusqu'à présent, s'efforceront de la rendre à la fois légère, économique et douce. Ils se proposent donc, de lui faire prendre la route de l'air, seul et infaillible moyen d'éviter les cahots et les ornieres, le dernier terme de sa course, sera la Chine et le Kamchatka: Son premier départ est irrévocablement fixé au 10 de Mai de l'an prochain 2440, le voyage sera au plus de 32 jours, le retour compris; mais jamais moins de 23, à cause des pertes de tems indispensables pour débarquer les passagers et les marchandises, le prix du trajet, sera de 30 Louis, avec la table du Capitaine: Chaque Voyageur ne pourra avoir plus de 6 quintaux pesant pour son Sac de nuit; le surplus sera payé à raison de 40ʟ par millier; On ne recevra jamais plus de 1349. passagers, le Calcul est de rigueur: Pour l'amusement des Voyageurs, il y aura des Musiciens qui tiendront Salle de Bal et Concert; ils se chargeront aussi moyennant 25 louis, de donner des Sérénades aux Villes qui se trouveront sur leur passage: Deux coups de Canon indiqueront l'arrivée de l'Orchestre au dessus de la Ville qui aura souscrit pour avoir de la musique: Enfin, la Table de Renvoy ci-après, indique tous les Détails qui constatent le merite et l'étendüe de cette entreprise déja mise à l'essai.

Table de Renvoy.

A. Le Globe...............	E. Promenades Publiques............	J. Tuyau pour écaler l'air inflamable	N. Casernes des Pompiers et Domestiques.
B. Voiles................	F. Ailes pour indiquer le vent......	K. Fanal composé de 300 Lampes à la Quinquet.	O. Tente pour l'Inspecteur des cordages.
C. Galerie...............	G. Musiciens, dans l'Orchestre......	L. Petit Ballon pour descendre les Voyageurs...	P. Armoiries du Capitaine et des Voyageurs.
D. Observatoire..........	H. Traits en échelle de corde.......	M. Tuyau général des Cheminées de la Voiture..	Q. La Voiture, appellée la grande Breloque.

Chapter 3

FIRST PRINCIPLES

Glider and dirigible design, the birth of aerodynamics, the search for power, transport potential, early gliding flights, Cayley, Degen, Phillips, Henson, Stringfellow.

'The whole problem is confined within these limits, viz – To make a surface support a given weight by the application of power to the resistance of air.'

SIR GEORGE CAYLEY, BT., 1809

The nineteenth century saw the Industrial Revolution in a Europe in which the patterns and habits of centuries were being changed by the impact of the railway and the steamship. It was a period of intense activity accompanied by invention and innovation, and of social, industrial and commercial change. The balloon and the parachute played no part in this, although they were clearly there to stay and interest in them continued unabated, while in the minds of many the idea of heavier-than-air flight was ridiculed. Heroes used the parachute or the balloon, cranks dreamed and spoke of heavier-than-air flight, children played with kites and toy windmills, while idiots tower jumped.

It was to be the work of the first half of the new century to inspire the public imagination with the possibilities of flight other than ballooning. While both varieties of the balloon were invented and caught the public imagination almost within a few months, the aeroplane was to require more than a century of solid scientific research and investigation, steady but often unspectacular progress, before it too could take to the air.

The age of ten years is considered to be impressionable, and certainly the events of 1783 made a profound impression on the young George Cayley (1773–1857), who, as Sir George Cayley, was to become in adult life one of the most inspired inventors ever produced by his native Yorkshire. It was none other than Sir George Cayley who brought to the whole question of flight the first truly scientific approach, coldly practical but brilliantly imaginative, and painstakingly foregoing any short cuts in order to lay solid foundations for future generations of would-be aviators to build upon. William Henson, with no mean reputation himself, hailed Cayley as 'The Father of Aerial Navigation', and time has enhanced rather than diminished this reputation.

A number of estimates of Cayley's main achievements exist, varying in some minor details but basically crediting him with having been responsible for:

> i) clarification of ideas on mechanical flight, while laying down the principles of heavier-than-air flight;
>
> ii) conducting experiments in aerodynamic research for flying purposes, including the pressures on surfaces at various angles of incidence, drawing attention to the importance of streamlining and outlining the body at least resistance, showing the movement of the centre of pressure of a surface in an airstream, and discovering that curved surfaces provide better lift than plane surfaces;
>
> iii) drawing attention to the effects of the dihedral angle for wings, and of a movable tailplane and rudder, while also considering the problems of

stability, weight control, the importance of the power/weight ratio and the need to discover a lightweight prime mover;

iv) the first design for a lightweight undercarriage through invention of the cycle-type tension wheel;

v) building the first man-carrying glider;

vi) suggesting jet reaction for propulsion and steering;

vii) suggesting the internal combustion engine for aircraft;

viii) using a whirling arm for aeronautical research for the first time, (although Smeaton had earlier used a whirling arm for research into the wind resistance of windmills);

ix) studying the basic principles of bird flight and achieving a genuine understanding of this;

x) suggesting the ideal configuration for an aircraft, with fuselage, undercarriage, mainplane and tailplane;

xi) designing the convertiplane, with a combination of fixed horizontal wing surfaces and vertical lift surfaces;

xii) suggesting water recovery for airships;

xiii) inventing the expansion air engine;

xiv) inventing the twisted rubber motor for model flying-machines;

xv) inventing the caterpillar tractor.

Some credit Cayley with using the first models for flying research, but, while it is probably true that he used the first heavier-than-air flying models, it must not be forgotten that the Montgolfiers and Charles dispatched small balloons before finally deciding to venture forth in large man-carrying aerostats. On the other hand, Cayley's proposal for water recovery of airships has something of an air of prophecy about it in the light of NASA's practice of recovering American manned space capsules from the sea. Interesting too, that Sir George Cayley, in so many ways Britain's answer to Leonardo da Vinci, although considerably more scientific than the Italian artist, should suggest the caterpillar tractor while da Vinci suggested a tank without caterpillar tracks. It could be said that the design of the tank as it emerged in the twentieth century incorporated the ideas of both men.

Like Da Vinci, Cayley was not purely a man of science, although he certainly excelled as such and covered an exceptionally wide field even by the standards of his day, in which specialisation was almost unknown – the examples of Stephenson, a locomotive engineer and a civil engineer, and of Brunel, who was a marine engineer as well, were not untypical. Cayley made contributions to electrical and optical science, and he was a keen agriculturalist, interested in land reclamation, as well as aeronautics. The other facets of Sir George Cayley could be seen in Sir George Cayley the poet, or the Whig politician, or the social reformer pressing for unemployment benefit, or even the founder of the original Regent Street Polytechnic in 1838. Many would be justifiably satisfied with a fraction of his achievements but, disregarding everything else, in the field of aeronautics alone he was the dominant figure for more than fifty years.

Cayley's first recorded work at the age of twenty-three was the construction of a helicopter model, in 1796, based on similar lines to that of Launoy and Bienvenu, although he did not at this stage know of their work. The results of tests with this model were not published until 1809, and although not a major step forward, the model was on the correct pattern of development which led in due course to the first practical helicopters. It is also known that, as early as 1799, he had formulated his basic fixed-wing glider design, although this was equipped with manually-operated flappers of doubtful usefulness. During the five years which followed he conducted numerous experiments with a whirling arm, obtaining results subsequently useful for aircraft wing design and leading to the first known heavier-than-air flying model in history in 1809. This was a five foot-long glider with a kite-form mainplane and a tailplane, and a movable weight fitted to alter the centre of gravity; this flew successfully.

Significant though this work was it only really marked the beginning for Cayley. Just how far ahead of his contemporaries he was can be judged by the way in which the tower jumpers were continually indulging in their almost lemming-like efforts. In 1801, at the age of seventy-two, a Frenchman, General Resnier de Goué, made a flying dive from the ramparts of Angoulême into the River Charente, escaping injury on that occasion but breaking a leg shortly afterwards when he attempted to repeat the escapade over dry land. The so-called Tailor of Ulm, Albrecht Berblinger, flapped miserably off the Adlerbastei at Ulm and into the Danube in 1811, using a replica of an ornithoptering device designed by a Swiss clock-maker, Jacob Degen, but without one vital component, a hydrogen balloon!

Jacob Degen (1756–1846) had in fact much to answer for. Cayley, so far ahead but perhaps at this early stage lacking confidence, thought of him as a serious rival. In fact the Englishman had nothing to fear. In 1809, Degen, who was living in Vienna at the time, built an ornithopter using flap-valves of the kind pioneered by Bauer in 1764, which closed on the downstroke and opened on the upstroke. Exhaustive tests with the device slung from a deadweight followed before he fitted a hydrogen balloon to the ornithopter, after which the lift of the balloon and of the ornithoptering motion resulted in a number of hops or jumps being achieved. Illustrations of the Degen balloon-ornithopter were widely circulated, but without any sign of the balloon, leading Cayley and Berblinger to believe that Degen had achieved man-powered heavier-than-air flight.

The results of Degen's work were threefold: Degen was injured after being attacked by disappointed spectators in Paris during October, 1812, because his performance did not come up to expectations; the Tailor of Ulm received an unasked for drenching; and Sir George Cayley was spurred into publication of his early work during 1809 and 1810 in *Nicholson's Journal*. Cayley's papers, 'On Aerial Navigation' were about 'the art of flying, or aerial navigation as I have chosen to term it for the sake of giving a little more dignity to a subject bordering upon the ludicrous in public estimation,' showing that Cayley at least had his feet firmly on the ground. He succeeded in his aim, partly because he was so aware of public opinion, and partly because he could produce tangible results, including the first full-sized glider in history, which made an unmanned flight in 1809, in what might be described as a tethered flight – using the glider in effect as a kite.

To be fair to Degen, he later undertook some useful work with clockwork-powered model helicopters. Another minor, but temporarily useful contribution to the development of heavier-than-air flight came from an English portrait painter, Thomas Walker, in 1810. Walker's treatise, *On the Art of Flying by Mechanical Means* promoted the cause of the man-powered ornithopter, and included a false claim of success for a fictitious design in which the pilot used arms and legs to flap the wings. However, a subsequent edition, published in 1831, was not without influence, proposing a tandem-wing ornithopter with fixed wings fore and aft, and a middle set of wings worked by the pilot. The tandem-wing concept was adopted by a number of those who followed, and notably by the unfortunate Samuel Langley.

A Count Adolphe de Lambertye produced a design for a giant ornithopter in 1818, in which it was intended that helicopters should ferry passengers and freight between the machine and the ground. This was never built. However, F. D. Artingstall, in 1829, built the first steam-powered ornithopters, both of which suffered the indignity of boiler explosions.

Against these somewhat clumsy efforts, Cayley's designs for a dirigible balloon, published in 1816 and offering either flapping or airscrew propulsion, had at least some air of reality about them.

Nevertheless, some success can be accorded to another Englishman at this time. George Pocock designed a kite-drawn road carriage in 1822, and this performed successfully on a run between Bristol and Marlborough in 1827. He also conducted experiments with man-carrying kites, eventually achieving sufficient success to risk an ascent by his daughter, Martha – probably the first woman to be carried by a kite and the mother of W.G. Grace, the cricketer.

Back on the ground, a carpenter, David Mayer, built a large man-powered helicopter which remained firmly earthbound in 1828, the year that the Italian, Vittoria Sarti designed, but failed to build, a contra-rotating helicopter.

For various reasons, in spite of designs by Meusnier and Cayley, design and construction of a successful dirigible balloon proved to be almost as elusive as the aeroplane itself, probably because of the structural techniques required and the lack of adequate powerplants. One such failure in what was eventually to become a thriving branch of aeronautics was the Lennox 'Eagle' airship of 1835, which was built for a London to Paris service and exhibited in London, but never became airborne. It would not have travelled far had it done so, depending on flappers for propulsion. A French counterpart was never completed.

Cayley himself suffered some failures. In 1809, he proposed an inverted-cone parachute, rather like an upside-down umbrella, which was intended to overcome the oscillations of the Garnerin parachute, first demonstrated in England in 1802. A water-colour artist, Robert Cocking (1777–37), at the age of sixty, undertook to make the first descent of an inverted-cone parachute. Oddly, he failed to conduct any tests before ascending with the parachute at the Royal Gardens, Vauxhall, London, on 24th July, 1837, under a balloon piloted by Charles Green. At a height of 5,000 feet, Cocking was released, and plunged to his death, the parachute disintegrating on the way. Although tests in the United States by John Wise, of Philadelphia, using a dog which descended with a Garnerin-style parachute and a cat which descended with a Cayley-designed parachute, later proved Cayley's theory to be correct, the inverted cone-parachute was abandoned, the oscillations eventually being overcome by use of different fabric for parachute construction.

However, perhaps Cayley could be forgiven one slip in a period which saw Georg Rebenstein of Nuremberg proposing a hot-air balloon which would collapse and glide to earth, and the production of worthless ornithopter designs by Doctor W. Miller in 1843, Duchesnay in 1845, Van Drieberg in 1845 and Marc Seguin in 1846. More successful, however, was the Austrian use of unmanned hot-air balloons to carry bombs against Venice in 1849; the first bombing raid in history.

Further evidence of Cayley's catholic interests appeared in an 1837 edition of the *Mechanics' Magazine*, in which he proposed a 'communicating centrifugal force to air by means of a hollow drum . . . means of getting a propelling power conveniently applicable in every direction' and a 'mouthpiece from which the air escapes, the momentum will be in the opposite direction.' This was taking Joseph Montgolfier's work a stage further, to the extent of proposing an elementary turbojet engine. Cayley had earlier suggested the expansion air engine in 1805, followed by a form of internal combustion engine using gunpowder, because no oil was available with a sufficiently low flashpoint. Later, he was to propose the use of wound elastic for the propulsion of model aeroplanes – a seemingly trivial matter, but it meant that flying test models could be built to determine the airworthiness of aircraft designs during the pioneering period.

A biplane convertiplane design of Cayley's published in 1843, is frequently described as being based on the work of Robert Taylor, although there were differences between the two designs, for example, the Taylor proposal for a monoplane rather than a biplane. That same year, Cayley also designed an ornithoptering glider and a design for vertical take-off flight, which appeared in an edition of the *Mechanics' Magazine*. Further designs for dirigible balloons followed, and by 1846 he had concluded that the practical difficulties of constructing a dirigible were less than those of constructing a working aeroplane, and successfully predicted that the dirigible would precede the aeroplane into the air.

The climax of Sir George Cayley's life, as far as his interest in aeronautics went, approached with the construction of a triplane glider in 1849. This made a number of trial flights in ballast, before carrying the ten-year-old son of a servant. In 1852, he published a glider design in the *Mechanics' Magazine*, with details of how to fly the completed craft. However, it was in 1853 that he sent his coachman, John Appleby, on a tentative flight across a valley near Brompton Hall, but, if a supposed eyewitness account is to be believed, the coachman's crash landing was not appreciated because he promptly threatened to resign from Cayley's service!

Recognition of Cayley's work first started to become apparent in the 1840s, along with the appearance of persons more qualified to be considered as rivals than Degen.

W.H. Phillips, in 1842, built a model steam-powered helicopter using rotor-tip steam-jets, somewhat on the lines of Hero of Alexandria's idea, but using a mixture of charcoal, nitre and gympsum as a power source. This was sufficiently successful for the machine to fly across two fields. The following year, another Englishman, Bourne, constructed and successfully tested a number of clockwork-powered helicopter designs, based on the Cayley and Launoy and Bienvenu designs. Yet another helicopter design appeared in 1845, although never built by its designer, one Cossuss, featuring a triple rotor system for lift and propulsion.

One of the most significant events of the mid-nineteenth century could be hailed as a success, even though by strict scientific criteria it must be considered a resounding failure. The success was due solely to the public interest which it inspired, although the design itself was not without merits and was the result of careful thought. It might be said that it was one of the first pieces of aeronautical apparatus to enjoy the benefits of an active, even, vast publicity machine. William Samuel Henson's 'Aerial Steam Carriage' design, produced in 1842, owed much to Cayley's work, of which Henson was an admirer, and was the first powered heavier-than-air flying machine in history to adopt a 'modern' configuration, with twin-pusher airscrews, high-wing monoplane and double-surfaced cambered wings, and tricycle undercarriage.

The intention was that a full-sized 'Ariel', as the machine was to be known, would use a 30 hp steam engine and have a wingspan of 150 feet, with take-off down-ramp to conserve power, and that regular airline services would be operated; this latter feature so caught the public imagination that for the next fifty years illustrations were to appear showing the 'Ariel' steaming across the skies, often en route to China.

Henson, with the somewhat strange background of the linen trade, was determined to operate regular air services as well as build the aeroplane, forming the 'Aerial Transit Company' with the assistance of his friend, John Stringfellow (1799–1883), an engineer also involved in the linen industry. Stringfellow's engineering background resulted in the engine for 'Ariel' being improved, but when a model was built, it only succeeded in trundling down-ramp during tests at Chard, Somerset, during 1845–7, possibly making a hop at the end, but certainly failing to become airborne. Henson sought comfort in marriage and emigration to the United States.

Stringfellow was less easily discouraged, however, developing the basic Henson design in a model with curved wings and flexible trailing edges, hoping that these features would provide increased stability. Rather than being launched down a ramp, the Stringfellow model was launched from an overhead wire, again at Chard, in 1848. Although the best powered design at that time, the model did not fly because it lacked stability and could not sustain the momentum of its launch, and eventually descended onto the ground at a lower level than its take-off point. Nevertheless, the achievement was real even if the result was basically a powered glide, and Stringfellow still did not feel inclined to follow Henson and abandon aeronautics completely, but instead took what might best be described as an extended leave.

Although the aeroplane was still a distant ambition by the mid-nineteenth century, the foundations of its development were being laid and, equally important, public attitudes to it were changing, if only from amusement to scepticism.

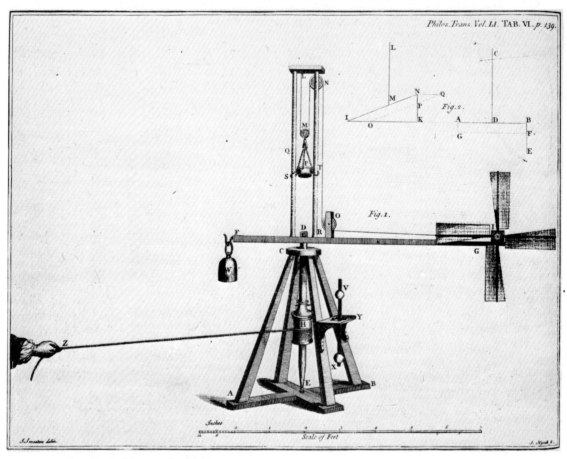

Philos. Trans. Vol. LI. TAB. VI. p. 139.

1 A detail of Smeaton's whirling
arm experiment, used during the
late eighteenth century for testing
the wind resistance of windmill
sails, and adopted by Sir George
Cayley for the testing of aerofoils.
(Photo: Science Museum, London).

2 Sir George Cayley, Bt., (1773–
1857) a member of a distinguished
Yorkshire family who became the
'Father of Aeronautics', crowding
into his life an intensive study of the
subject along with a keen interest
in social reform, land reclamation
and politics, amongst other things,
as well as the invention of the
caterpillar tractor. (Photo: Science
Museum, London).

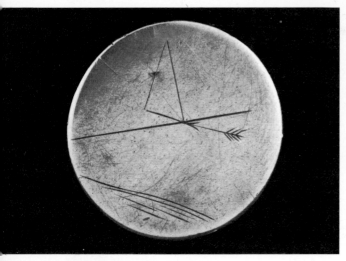

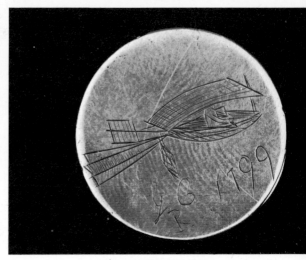

3 A silver disc, dated 1799, on which Sir George Cayley has shown the forces of lift, drag and thrust, with . . .

4 on the other side, an initialled sketch of a fixed-wing glider with tailplane and flappers. (Crown Copyright, Science Museum, London).

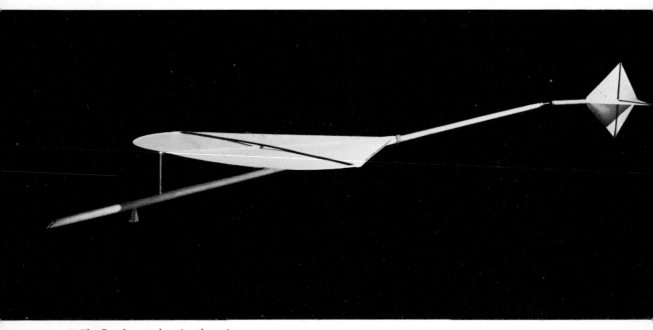

5 The first known heavier-than-air flying model; this is a reproduction of the Cayley kite-glider of 1809, which featured a kite as a mainplane, a tailplane and a movable weight to alter the centre of gravity. The original made a number of successful glides. (Crown Copyright, Science Museum, London).

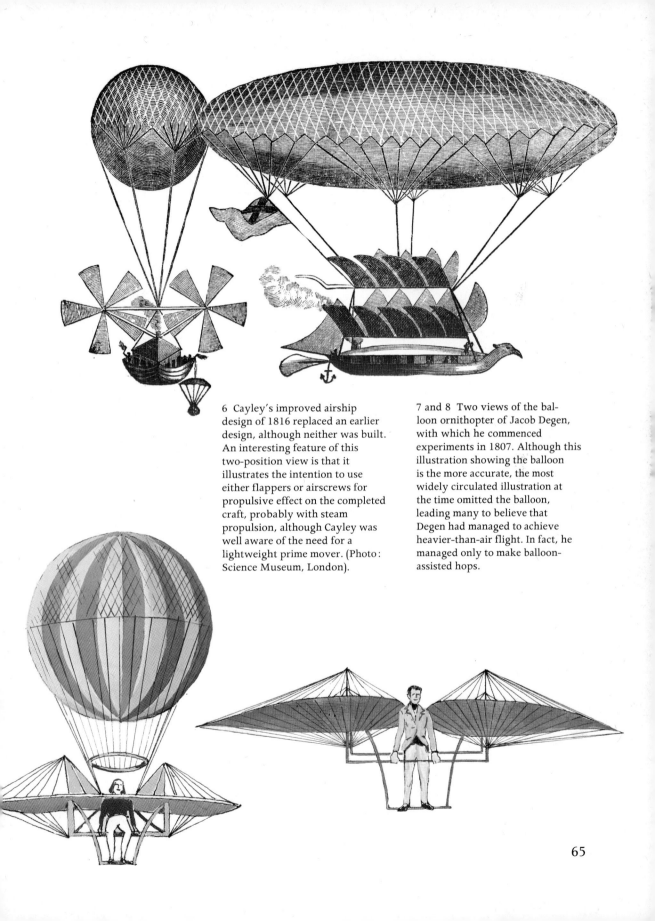

6 Cayley's improved airship design of 1816 replaced an earlier design, although neither was built. An interesting feature of this two-position view is that it illustrates the intention to use either flappers or airscrews for propulsive effect on the completed craft, probably with steam propulsion, although Cayley was well aware of the need for a lightweight prime mover. (Photo: Science Museum, London).

7 and 8 Two views of the balloon ornithopter of Jacob Degen, with which he commenced experiments in 1807. Although this illustration showing the balloon is the more accurate, the most widely circulated illustration at the time omitted the balloon, leading many to believe that Degen had managed to achieve heavier-than-air flight. In fact, he managed only to make balloon-assisted hops.

65

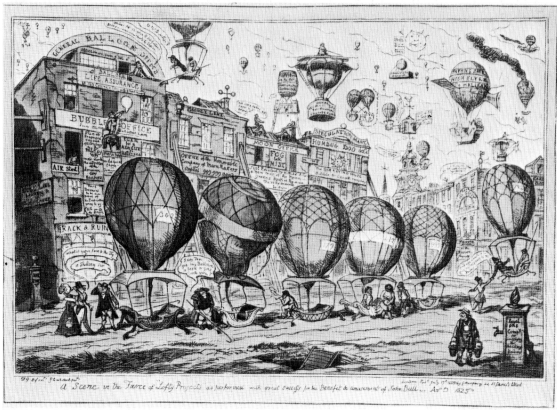

A Scene in the Farce of Lofty Projects as performed with great success for the Benefit & amusement of John Bull. Anno D. 1825.

9 Inevitably, the activities of the balloonists and their more wild fantasies attracted comment, one of the more interesting being this cartoon by George Cruikshank in 1825. Balloons are shown in use for every conceivable purpose, one of the more plausible being balloon-cabs for use in London with one 'driver' about to pick up a fare and another seeking a 'feed o'gas' for his vehicle. (Photo: Science Museum, London).

10 The death of Madame Blanchard, widow of the famous balloonist and herself an active participant in the sport. Her main activity was the making of exhibition ascents, with the added attraction of dropping fireworks on small parachutes from the balloon. On this occasion, in 1819, the fire used to light the fireworks spread to the balloon envelope causing a rapid descent. All might have been well but for the fact that the balloon landed on a roof top spilling Madame Blanchard from the gondola to fall to the ground below.

11 One of a number of cartoons produced around 1828 and featuring a Mr Golightly mounted on a steam-powered rocket. Interesting features, apart from this vision of rocket flight about a hundred years before the first experiments with rocket-powered aircraft, include the realisation that control could be effected by swivelling the efflux. (Photo: Science Museum, London).

12 A further development on the Golightly theme, but this time with wings. Headgear seems to be dispensible for rocket riders, as does the atmosphere in this illustration of an 'Elopement Extraordinary, or Jack and his Lassie on a Matrimonial Excursion to the Moon on the New Aerial Machine'. (Photo: Science Museum, London).

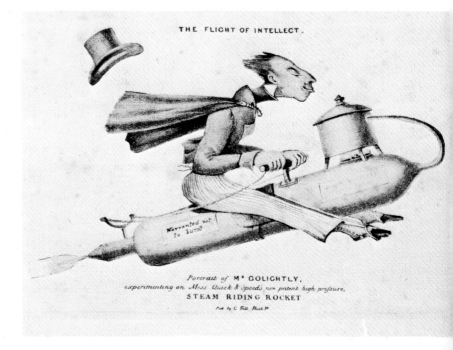

THE FLIGHT OF INTELLECT.

Portrait of Mr GOLIGHTLY,
experimenting on Miss Quick & Speed's *new patent high pressure*,
STEAM RIDING ROCKET

Elopement Extraordinary, or Jack and his Lassie on a Matrimonial Excursion to the Moon, on the New Aerial Machine.

13 Paris to St Petersburg in one hour – a distance of 1,400 miles! A German version of Golightly. (Photo: Science Museum, London).

14 The Englishman, George Pocock, produced his first kite carriage design in 1822, and a successful road trial was undertaken between Bristol and Marlborough in 1827, which is the theme of this illustration of the kite carriage or 'Char-Volant'. It is doubtful whether this illustration can be taken as a true record of the occasion, since artistic licence has extended to adding other kite carriages to the scene, and it might also be wondered whether in fact larger kites than those shown were used. (Photo: Science Museum, London).

15 A hopeful design for an airship by Pauly and Egg, and first published in 1835 as the 'Dolphin'. It was never built, which must be considered as a fortunate saving of useless effort! (Photo: Science Museum, London).

16 The first airship to be built in the United Kingdom, the Lennox 'Eagle', which was completed in 1835 and exhibited in London. It was intended that it should inaugurate a London to Paris service in August of that year, but the 'Eagle' never became airborne, and the flappers would have proved to be ineffectual had it done so. The complementary French craft was never completed. (Photo: Science Museum, London).
▼

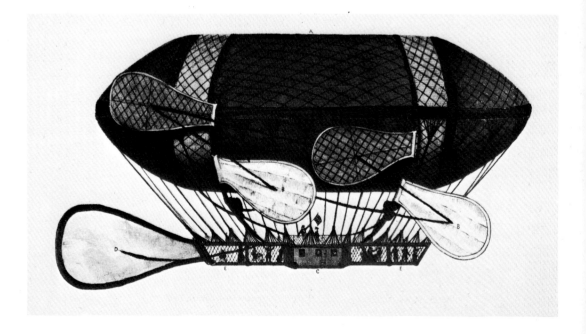

ROYAL GARDENS, VAUXHALL.

GRAND DAY FÈTE,

On MONDAY, the 24th of JULY, 1837.

Extraordinary Novelty and Combined Attraction!

ASCENT IN THE ROYAL NASSAU BALLOON

BY MR. GREEN,

AND DESCENT IN A NEWLY-INVENTED

PARACHUTE,

BY MR. COCKING.

The Proprietors of Vauxhall have the satisfaction to announce that they are enabled to present to the Public another grand improvement connected with the Science of Aerostation; viz. a PARACHUTE of an entirely Novel Construction, by which a perfectly safe and easy descent may be made from any height in the Atmosphere attainable by a Balloon.

Mr. COCKING, a gentleman of great scientific acquirements, having, many years since, witnessed the descent of M. Garnerin, (the only one ever made in England,) was forcibly struck with the danger to which that gentleman was exposed on account of some error in the construction of his machine; and, after several years spent in numerous experiments, has succeeded in discovering the faults in M. Garnerin's instrument, and also in producing

AN ENTIRELY NEW PARACHUTE,

which is allowed by all who have seen it, to be constructed on unerring principles. The form is that of

An Inverted Cone 107 Feet in Circumference!

which, during the Descent, is quite free from oscillation; and as it will be in its proper form previous to the Ascent, it is not liable to the objection of falling several hundred feet without expanding, which was the case with the Parachute of the old form.

MR. COCKING WILL MAKE HIS FIRST DESCENT
ON MONDAY NEXT, JULY 24.

The great power of the Royal Nassau Balloon has afforded the means of making an experiment with the above-named Machine, which, from its great weight, would be impossible with any other Balloon hitherto constructed.

The plan adopted by M. Garnerin was to ascend alone and detach the Parachute from the Balloon, which having no person to conduct it fell in some very distant part, and was either lost or destroyed; but Mr. GREEN has undertaken to ascend in the Nassau Balloon, and to liberate the Parachute himself, a feat never before attempted by any Aeronaut.

THE PARACHUTE WILL BE EXHIBITED PREVIOUS TO ITS ASCENT.

In order to render this Fète more than usually attractive, the Proprietors intend giving a variety of Amusements during the Afternoon, the principal of which are—

A CONCERT in the Open Orchestra
A DRAMATIC PIECE in the Theatre, which will be lighted as at Night
The Extraordinary Performance of M. LATOUR, M. DE LA VIGNE, & their Sons
THE YEOMANRY AND QUADRILLE BANDS, &c. &c. &c.

AND A VARIETY OF OTHER ENTERTAINMENTS.

Doors will be opened at One; & the Ascent at Five.

The Descent will be made as nearly over the Gardens as possible.—ADMISSION, 2s. 6d.

VISITORS ARE REQUESTED TO COME EARLY.

The Admission to the Evening Entertainments will be as usual.——Parties can Dine in the Gardens.

[Balne, Printer, 38, Gracechurch Street.

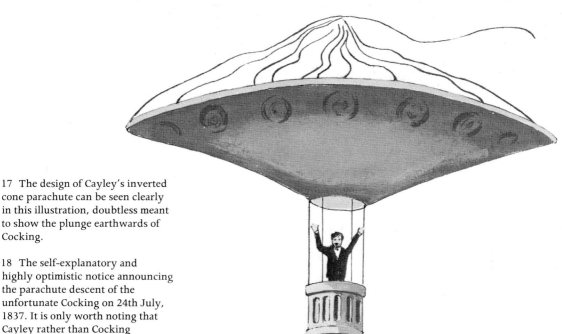

17 The design of Cayley's inverted cone parachute can be seen clearly in this illustration, doubtless meant to show the plunge earthwards of Cocking.

18 The self-explanatory and highly optimistic notice announcing the parachute descent of the unfortunate Cocking on 24th July, 1837. It is only worth noting that Cayley rather than Cocking conceived this form of parachute, and that Cocking was an artist rather than a man of science. (Photo: Science Museum, London).

19 This triple rotor helicopter design by Cossus appeared in 1845 but was never built. The centre rotor was to provide lift, while the two smaller rotors were to propel and steer the machine.

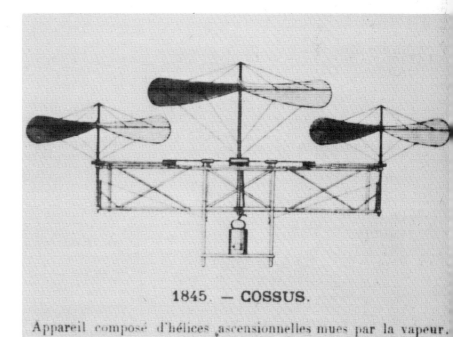

1845 — COSSUS.

Appareil composé d'hélices ascensionnelles mues par la vapeur.

20 A model of Sir George Cayley's 'Aerial Carriage', the design for which was published in the *Mechanics' Magazine* for 8th April, 1843. In effect, a biplane converti-plane, allegedly based on an earlier design by Robert Taylor for a monoplane convertiplane. The twin pusher-propellers for forward flight can be seen behind the 'rotary wings'. The design was never built. (Crown Copyright, Science Museum, London).

21 The front cover of the *Mechanics' Magazine* for 25th September, 1852, showing Sir George Cayley's 'Governable Parachutes'. The design was really that for the first pilot-controllable glider, which, if built, would have been launched from a balloon. The kite influence can still be seen, but this design can be credited with considerable importance and a strong likelihood of success, although it was largely ignored and quickly forgotten. (Photo: Science Museum, London).

▶

𝕸𝖊𝖈𝖍𝖆𝖓𝖎𝖈𝖘' 𝕸𝖆𝖌𝖆𝖟𝖎𝖓𝖊,

MUSEUM, REGISTER, JOURNAL, AND GAZETTE.

No. 1520.]   SATURDAY, SEPTEMBER 25, 1852.   [Price 3*d*., Stamped 4*d*.

Edited by J. C. Robertson, 166, Fleet-street.

SIR GEORGE CAYLEY'S GOVERNABLE PARACHUTES.

Fig. 2.

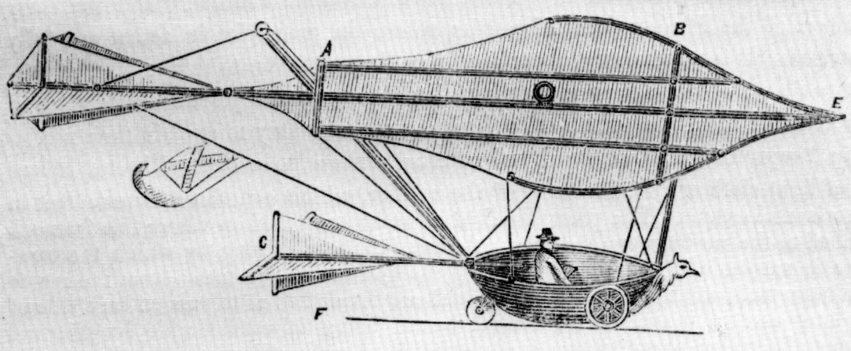

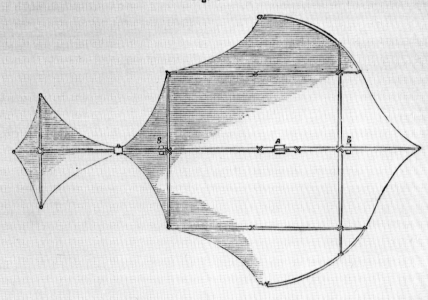

Fig. 1.

22 William Samuel Henson
(1812–88) was the first to recognise
the value of the work undertaken
by his contemporary and fellow
countryman, Cayley, whom he
described as 'The Father of Aerial
Navigation'. Henson's own
contribution to aeronautical
development was far from
insignificant, but he quickly lost
heart in spite of the support of his
friend, John Stringfellow. (Photo:
Science Museum, London).

23 Henson's 'Ariel' flies over all of
the signs of the industrial revolution
on a service of the 'Aerial Transit
Company' – the first airline, although
it never became operational. This and
other evocative illustrations were the
result of the endeavours of Henson's
brilliant publicity agent, Frederick
Marriott, who so succeeded in im-
planting the 'Ariel' in the public
imagination that illustrations like this
appeared throughout the nineteenth
century. (Photo: Science Museum, London).

24 A different view of the 'Ariel'
in flight, with a Red Ensign
fluttering proudly. At a time when
photography was only just
appearing, engravings such as this
still had considerable impact, and
even today Henson's design stops
short of the ridiculous. (Photo:
Science Museum, London). ▶

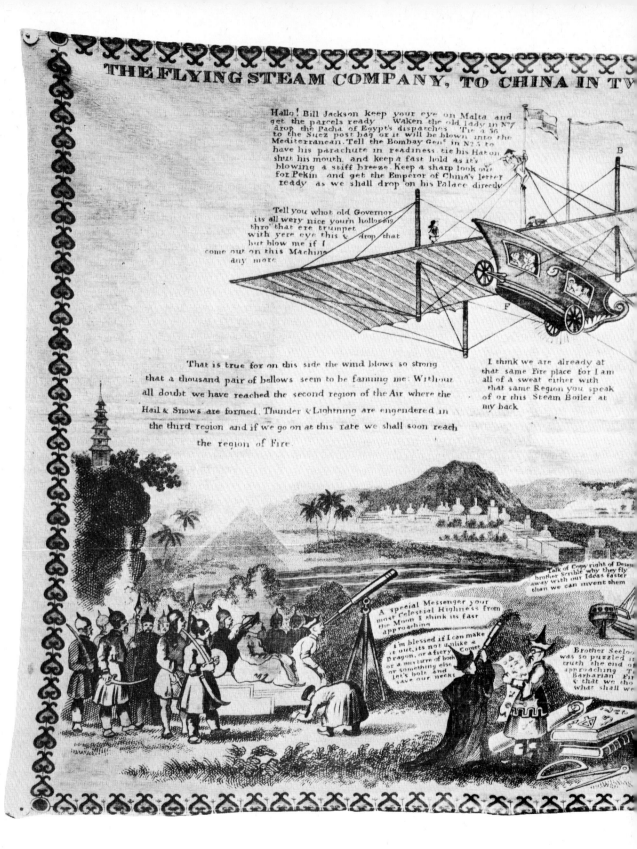

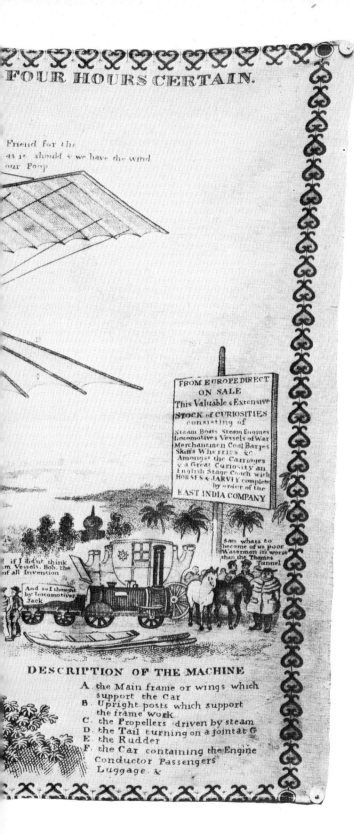

FOUR HOURS CERTAIN.

Friend for the
as it should s we have the wind
our Poop

FROM EUROPE DIRECT
ON SALE
This Valuable & Extensive
STOCK of CURIOSITIES
consisting of
Steam Boats Steam Engines
Locomotives Vessels of War
Merchantmen Coal Barges
Skiffs Wherries &c
Amongst the Carriages
a Great Curiosity an
English Stage Coach with
HORSES & JARVEY complete
by order of the
EAST INDIA COMPANY

Sam whats to
become of us poor
Watermen its worse
than the Thames
Tunnel

if I didn't think
m Vessels, Bob, the
of all Invention

And so I thought
by Locomotives
Jack

DESCRIPTION OF THE MACHINE

A the Main frame or wings which
support the Car
B Upright posts which support
the frame work
C the Propellers driven by steam
D the Tail turning on a joint at G
E the Rudder
F the Car containing the Engine
Conductor Passengers
Luggage &

25 John Stringfellow (1799–1883)
an engineer and a friend of Henson,
took over where the latter left off.
A brilliant engineer, Stringfellow
enjoyed little more success than
Henson, and an attempt by his son,
F.J.Stringfellow, to continue this
aspect of the 'family business' also
seems to have been doomed to
failure. (Photo: Science Museum,
London).

26 The 'Ariel' was not above some
mild caricature, as on this
handkerchief. Obviously, the
'Empire' routes were very much in
mind, and China also would seem
to have held a fascination for this
as for other projects. (Crown
Copyright, Science Museum,
London).

27 Obviously acting as a drawing room conversation piece! This model was Stringfellow's development of Henson's original design, and the curved wings and movable tail were thought to provide stability necessary for flight to be achieved. Tests in 1848 resulted in a powered glide from the overhead launching wire. (Photo: Science Museum, London).

28 An illustration looking forward to a 'Paris-Alger' dirigible service. The influence which ship design had on thoughts about airships can be seen. (Photo: Science Museum, London).

MARCH of INTELLECT

29 'The March of Intellect', meant to be a despairing look at the advancement of science, judging from the remark, 'Lord, how this world improves as we grow older'. Developments in tube railways and in steam-powered road vehicles are satirised along with those of aeronautics, although close scrutiny reveals that not all of the fantasy can be counted as undesirable, even if impractical! (Photo: Science Museum, London).

Chapter 4

FALTERING STEPS

First dirigible flight, aerial surveys, aeronautical societies, glider flights, interest in propulsion, rocket and jet aircraft designs, Giffard, Le Bris, Du Temple, Nadar, D'Esterno, Butler, Edwards, Wenham, Stringfellow, Marriott.

'I suppose we shall soon travel by air-vessels; make air instead of sea-voyages; and at length find our way to the moon, in spite of the want of atmosphere.'

LORD BYRON, 1822

It is to Sir George Cayley's credit that he made the idea of heavier-than-air flight respectable, although cynics were numerous and continued to be so even, in some cases, until well after the Wright Brothers' flights of 1903. This is, if anything, a fair indication of the prejudices which the pioneers had to overcome, for if the technical problems alone were not enough, the barriers in people's minds had also to be tackled. The two are not unrelated, for it can take a brave mind to concentrate on a problem which many see as laughable.

On a more constructive note, Cayley had obviously dominated the first half of the nineteenth century as far as aeronautics was concerned, and during this period he had correctly predicted the course of development for the second half of the century. In this he realised that the problems of the dirigible were less than those of the aeroplane, but the real problem for both was, and would remain, the need for a lightweight but efficient source of power.

It was because of this that the period which followed had in some respects an astonishing air of anti-climax about it. The great man had taken the science of aeronautics so far along the road to success, indeed the science was largely his own invention, but he could not take it far enough. Those who came immediately after Cayley were so near, yet so far from their goal. Few could compare with the brilliance of the Yorkshire baronet, but there was a tendency still for many to pursue unrealistic theories, although the disappearance of the tower jumpers could be considered a step forward.

For the first time, almost as much attention was to be given to the search for power, the discovery of a suitable powerplant, as to aircraft and airship design. This interest marked the entire second half of the century.

Already accomplished balloonists by the turn of the century, the aeronauts of the first half of the nineteenth century were not content to sit around waiting for the arrival of the aeroplane or even the airship. In 1836, the first long-distance balloon flight from the United Kingdom was undertaken by Robert Holland MP, and Monck Mason, who ascended on 7th November from Vauxhall Gardens in London, and travelled for more than 400 miles to descend the following day at Weilberg, in the German Duchy of Nassau Originally named the 'Royal Vauxhall Balloon', their craft was renamed the 'Great Balloon of Nassau', or 'Royal Nassau Balloon', and it was from this that Cocking made his ill-fated parachute descent in 1837. Odd to notice that Holland, like his contemporary Cayley, was a politician, for certainly it has not proved possible to send the honourable members into space with quite the same ease!

Aerostation remained fashionable, but it was also becoming a tool, if not quite a workhorse in the same sense that this term has been applied to certain well-loved aircraft. HMS *Assistance*, searching in the Canadian arctic for the ill-fated Sir John Franklin expedition in 1850, launched a series of small unmanned hydrogen balloons, carrying bundles of messages giving the ship's position.

The American Civil War was not so far ahead, and balloons were to be used by the Unionist Army for observation duties between 1861 and 1866. One of the most important balloonists of the Civil War was Professor Thaddeus Lowe, who made frequent ascents in his balloon, 'Intrepid', both on reconnaissance duties, including those for the Battle of Fair Oaks, in Virginia, during 1862, and for making what might be described as the first aerial maps from sketches of Virginia which he made from his balloon during December, 1862. As in the War of the French Revolution, the balloons were usually tethered to prevent them from straying over enemy territory.

One of the peculiarities of aeronautical development has been the way in which first one country and then another has taken the lead, with the initiative being passed from one to another. This continues to the present day with, at most, the lead being held by one country for twenty years or so. The predominance of Sir George Cayley, lasting for more than fifty years, was the exception, and even during the period immediately before his death, while he was conducting the first glider flight, inventing the rubber motor, designing a controllable glider, and experimenting with his aerial top, the French were regaining the position they had held in the late eighteenth century.

The possibilities of the ornithopter continued to intrigue many, including a Frenchman, Aubaud, who produced an ornithopter-helicopter design in 1851. Another design, which could hardly be described as practical, also came from France some three years later, consisting of an ornithopter in which the pilot lowered the wings, and a rubber motor raised them! Neither design appears to have been built.

Some real significance can, however, be attached to the first consistent French aeroplane design in 1853 by Michel Loup. This was also the first of the bird-form monoplanes which seem to have been particularly favoured by French designers from 1850 onwards. Other features included an airscrew in each wing and a tricycle undercarriage. The Loup design was not built, although in 1856 Viscount Carlingford designed a Loup-type monoplane with a single steam-powered tractor propeller, and a model of this flew successfully as a kite in Ireland. A rubber-powered model by Pierre Jullien in 1858 flew for some forty feet, and this was the first French-built powered flying model.

In spite of the Lennox 'Eagle' airship and the work by Sir George Cayley, it is perhaps appropriate that the first dirigible, or navigable, airship to take to the air should have come from the country of the Montgolfiers and Charles, Blanchard and Meusnier. This was the work of Henri Giffard (1825–82), and its significance also lies in the fact of its being the first application of power to man-carrying flight. Like Cayley, Giffard was not solely devoted to aeronautics, and it was the invention of the steam injector, and the subsequent royalties he earned from it, which enabled him to pursue his plans for an airship. A weird and unwieldy craft, the Giffard airship was powered by a single-cylinder, 3 hp, steam engine, which was slung under a beam running the whole length of the hydrogen-filled envelope, thus spreading the weight of the powerplant and pilot over the primitive structure.

Giffard's airship was far from being a practical craft. It ascended, carrying its designer-builder, from the Hippodrome in Paris on 24th September, 1852, and then flew the seventeen miles to Trappes at a speed which never exceeded five miles per hour – less than half that of a stage coach and even further below the speeds being attained by the railways at that time. Only minor deviations from the direction of the wind were possible with the Giffard, and the airship could not navigate a circle with its meagre power source.

An Englishman, James Nye, considered that the problems of finding a suitable airship powerplant could be solved by the use of rockets, but there are no records of rocket propulsion being applied to an airship at this time (this was still during 1852) or since.

Louis Charles Letur built an interesting parachute-type glider in 1853, in which the pilot sat beneath an adjustable canopy wing and worked two large flappers. This was the first heavier-than-air flying-machine to become airborne when it was first test-launched from a balloon that same year. A number of demonstration launchings followed in both France and England, and it was during one of the latter that disaster struck on 27th June, 1854. Letur, after being launched in his apparatus at Tottenham, near London, discovered a fault and attempted to make an emergency landing, but instead crashed into some trees and suffered injuries from which he died eight days later.

A more fortunate contemporary of the brave Letur was the sea captain, Jean Marie Le Bris (1808–72). Many sea captains of the period were still keen naturalists, although perhaps less so than their brethren of a generation earlier, and Le Bris used his studies of the albatross to design a bird-form monoplane glider, which he subsequently built. A novel feature of the design, for the time, was the seating of the pilot in a fuselage cockpit. The first Le Bris glider was launched from a cart drawn at speed along a road near Trefeuntec, in France, during 1856. The first flight resulted in a short glide, while the second ended with the glider crashing and Le Bris breaking a leg.

It was also at this time that a French naval officer, Félix du Temple (1823–

90), first came to prominence, although in due course his contribution to aeronautical history was to be greater than that of Le Bris. Du Temple built a model aeroplane with which he conducted a number of experiments, sometimes assisted by his brother Louis, during 1857–8, initially using a clockwork motor but later replacing this with a steam engine. This model was the first powered heavier-than-air flying-machine to be able to sustain itself in flight. Greatly encouraged by this, Du Temple built the first full-sized powered flying-machine, a monoplane with dihedral and reverse sweep to the wings, a tailplane with rudder, and a retractable undercarriage, with a single tractor propeller driven by a steam engine. Strangely, no attempt was made at flight for some years.

Very much on the edge of this activity, an Irish priest, Father Cordner, designed, built, and then tested, a large multiple man-carrying kite for coastal rescue work. It is not known whether this novel idea was ever of any practical value, but it is unlikely. Multiple man-carrying kites have made very little progress, although there have been many examples of single man-carrying kites which have been successful within their limitations.

A resurgence of ornithoptering activity seems to have occurred during the early 1860s in England, France and Germany. One of the ornithopterists was the Englishman, Smythies, who in 1860 designed a machine with fixed wings for lift and steam-driven flapping wings for propulsion, while the centre of gravity could be adjusted by moving the pilot's seat. The Alsatian, J.J. Bourçart, built an unsuccessful man-powered ornithopter in 1863, and during the following year, Struvé and Telescheff designed another man-powered ornithopter, with no less than five sets of wings which were supposed to provide stability.

More promising was the Vicomte Ponton d'Amecourt's interest in helicopters. The first of these was a contra-rotating design, patented in 1861 and built as a model in 1863, which was steam-powered and a failure; although other models which followed, using clockwork motors, performed tolerably well, including one with a parachute to return the machine to earth after the motor wound down.

Perhaps not directly connected with the vast business of getting mankind into the air, it is nevertheless worth noting that the word 'aviation', meaning powered heavier-than-air flight, was first coined in 1863 by a Frenchman, Gabriel de la Landelle, who also coined the word aviator (l'aviateur!) at about the same time. De la Landelle's contributions to aviation science were less worthy, being almost solely confined to a helicopter design, resembling nothing so much as a mixed sail and steam ship, but with multiple airscrews mounted on the masts instead of sails. One can only speculate on whether or not this influenced Jules Verne when writing his inspired *Clipper of the Clouds*, which appeared in 1886.

Still in a literary vein, the first aeronautical journal in the world, *L'Aeronaute*, was produced in 1864 by Felix Tourmachon, who usually rejoiced in the strange title of Nadar. Unfortunately, *L'Aeronaute* ran for only five issues, although it was restarted in 1868 by Abel Hureau de Villeneuve as *L'Aeronaute: Bulletin mensuel de la Navigation aérienne*, and in this form appeared regularly until 1912.

A more successful brainchild of Nadar's was the '*Société d'Encouragement pour la Navigation Aérienne au Moyens d'Appareils plus lourds que l'Air*', formed in 1863, and which flourished. One of the first encouraging steps taken was the simplification of the title to the '*Société d'Aviation*', for which one must be heartily thankful to De la Landelle! An earlier French organisation, and the first aeronautical organisation in the world, had been the '*Société Aérostatique et Météorologique de France*', formed in 1852 and which merged with Nadar's aviation society in 1863, becoming the '*Société Français de Navigation Aérienne*': The term aviation would hardly have been appropriate for an organisation also covering aerostation (i.e. lighter-than-air flight).

Another of the French bird-form advocates, Count Ferdinand Charles Honoré Phillipe d'Esterno (1806–83), published his *Du Vol des Oiseux* in 1864, drawing attention to the soaring, rather than the gliding, flight of birds. His work was spoiled by the absence of any study of lateral control, and indeed most of his thoughts on control, like those of Smythies, consist of moving the centre of gravity of the glider. A glider design by d'Esterno, although never built, had the interesting features of variable-incidence and variable-dihedral, preceding the LTV F-8 Crusader by about a hundred years on the former. A countryman of D'Esterno, Louis Pierre Mouillard (1834–97) also built a glider in 1865, and although this only made a few tentative glides, he was later to make some important contributions to knowledge of soaring flight.

Jean Marie Le Bris built and tested his second albatross-form glider in 1868, and although no record exists of the craft in the air (it is supposed to have flown), it must have been one of the first flying-machines to be photographed.

Almost as if attempting to run before they could even walk, the French aeronauts at this time included amongst their number many believers in jet and rocket propulsion. The first design for a jet-propelled aeroplane was by Charles de Louvrie, whose '*Aeronave*' design was first published in 1863, reappearing in modified form two years later, but never built. That some sound thought had gone into the design can be judged by the explanation that propulsion would result from the burning of 'vapourised petroleum oil'. Also credited to France, the country of its original patent, although originating with a Russian army officer, Nicholas de Telescheff, was another jet design, this time for a delta-wing monoplane with propulsion effected by vapourised liquid, compressed and mixed with air before ignition to provide thrust.

Meanwhile the British aeronauts were coming back to the fore. J. W. Butler and E. Edwards in 1867 patented their delta-wing design, the first in history, which in appearance closely resembled a schoolboy's paper aeroplane. This was described as being intended for propulsion by inflammable vapour and air, steam, or even by compressed air. They followed this with a delta-biplane design during that same year, with a three-bladed pusher-propeller rotated by a jet efflux from the tips of the blades. In some ways a Hero of Alexandria solution, it is also worth remembering that the idea of rotor tip jets, or of ducting jet efflux to rotor tips, has been applied to experimental VTOL aircraft in recent years.

Then, at last, in 1866, the British formed the Aeronautical Society (today the Royal Aeronautical Society), thus fulfilling a frustrated ambition of the then late Sir George Cayley. The new society got off to a promising start, with a paper 'On Aerial Locomotion' by Francis Herbert Wenham (1824–1908), a marine engineer who had built a number of gliders in 1858–9, including a model and two full-sized man-carrying machines, with which he had experimented quietly, but effectively, to prove his theories about wing design.

Wenham would have been an outstanding figure, indeed he was, but for the fact that he was standing very much in Cayley's shadow. Nevertheless, he took Cayley's findings on the cambered wing further, after an exhaustive study of the characteristics of bird wings, which he discovered to be cambered and with a thicker section on the leading edge than on the trailing edge, and drawing most of the lift from the front part of the wing. His gliders were remarkable for having no less than five planes or wings, leading to the biplane, triplane and multiplane of later years, and an interesting feature was the prone position of the pilot during flight.

The Aeronautical Society may have started later than its French counterparts, although it has been considerably longer-lived, but it can take the credit for holding the first aeronautical exhibition, a forerunner of the aviation meetings and airshows of more recent years, at the Crystal Palace in London in 1868. One of the attractions was a display of powerplants, which at this time included many unlikely specimens, although the age of the internal combustion engine was drawing near; a forerunner had been Lenoir's gas engine of 1860.

One of the items in the exhibition was a steam-powered triplane model built by John Stringfellow, Henson's former associate and friend. This proved to be even less successful aerodynamically than his earlier models, although, like the 'Ariel', it caught the imagination of press and public alike, and had a considerable influence on subsequent design. However, it is pleasing to know that the elderly Stringfellow also exhibited one of his small steam engines, for which he won a prize of £100.

Another of Henson's associates – it is tempting to call them accomplices, but that would hardly be a fair description – surfaces during the late 1860s in California. This was none other than Frederick Marriott, the highly skilful publicity agent for the 'Aerial Transit Company' of 1842–3. In 1869, Marriott designed and built a steam-powered airship with the unusual feature of a wing, built out from the gas bag and running for approximately half its length, and a tailplane. This is supposed to have made a flight, even though the machine was heavier-than-air. There has been considerable debate over Marriott's claim, and perhaps the truth of the matter was that, like the Degen balloon-ornithopter, the Marriott aeroplane-airship probably made a number of hops once power was applied.

It is, perhaps, worth mentioning another exhibitor at the 1868 Crystal Palace exhibition: J.M.Kaufman, an engineer from Glasgow, who built a steam-powered model ornithopter with a locomotive-type funnel, two pairs of flappers and a quadruplane wing. Displayed at the exhibition, it flapped itself to pieces on a subsequent test without becoming airborne at any time.

In 1868 and 1870, M.P.W.Boulton and Robert Harte independently proposed differing types of ailerons for aeroplane control. Little credit can be attributed to Boulton, whose ailerons were of a type which would have given rise to more problems than they could solve, but the Harte ailerons held promise although they were neglected by contemporary aeroplane designers.

A rising star was a young German, Otto Lilienthal (1848–96), who had already started his aeronautical experiments in 1867, initially with a six flapper ornithopter which he tested against a counter-weight. However, it was to be some years still before Lilienthal was to come into prominence with his successful hang-gliders.

The science of aeronautics in 1870 was only a little closer to the practical airship and the first flight of an aeroplane than it had been in the middle of the century. However, the minor steps forward which had been taken, together with the increasing interest in propulsion, did at least mean that some progress was being maintained. The real momentum was yet to build up.

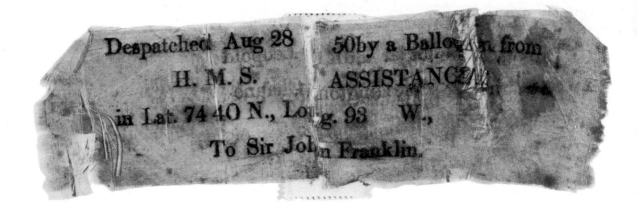

Despatched Aug 28   50 by a Balloon from
H. M. S.   ASSISTANCE
in Lat. 74 40 N., Long. 93 W.,
To Sir John Franklin.

W. E. Earl.   Norwich.

THE NASSAU BALLOON,

As it Ascended from Norwich on Thursday September 24th, 1840, with the following Gentlemen,—R. Crawshay, Esq.
F. Crawshay, Esq.   E. Crawshay, Esq.   N. Bacon, Esq.   W. Andrews.   W. Shalders, and Mr. Green.

1 A balloon message stamped on blue paper. This was one of many such messages dispatched from HMS *Assistance* while in the Canadian Arctic in 1850, searching for survivors of the ill-fated Sir John Franklin Expedition. The messages were tied in small bundles to a length of slow-burning fuse attached to small balloons, to ensure an even spread of the messages giving the ship's position over as wide an area as possible. (Photo: Science Museum, London).

2 The 'Great Balloon of Nassau', or 'Royal Nassau Balloon', which made the record flight from Vauxhall to Weilberg in 1836, and from which Cocking jumped in 1837. It is seen here on an ascent from Norwich, on 24th September, 1840. One of the occupants in the picture is Charles Green, who piloted the balloon at the time of Cocking's descent. (Photo: Science Museum, London).

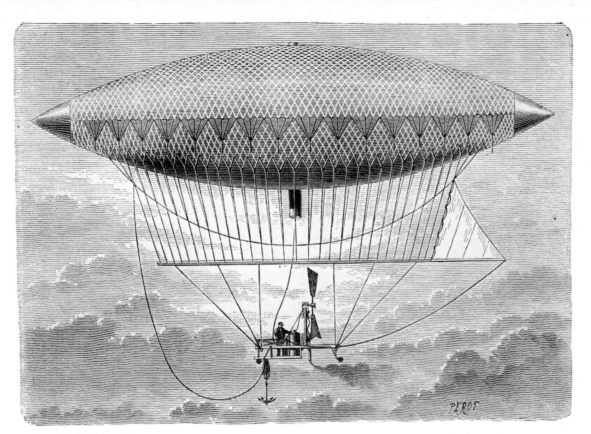

3 The Giffard airship of 1852, which made a tentative voyage from Paris to Trappes on 24th September, 1852. Although the first airship to become airborne, the Giffard was far from being a practical craft, mainly because it was under-powered. (Photo: Science Museum, London).

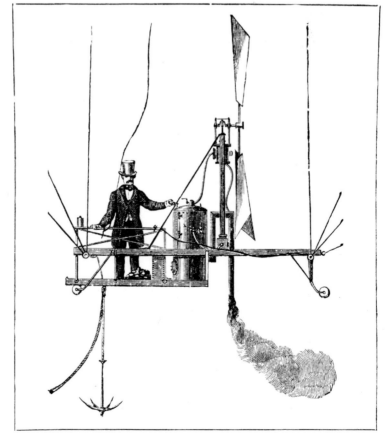

4 A detail of the gondola of the Giffard airship, showing Henri Giffard by the small steam engine which was supposed to power the airship. (Photo: Science Museum, London).

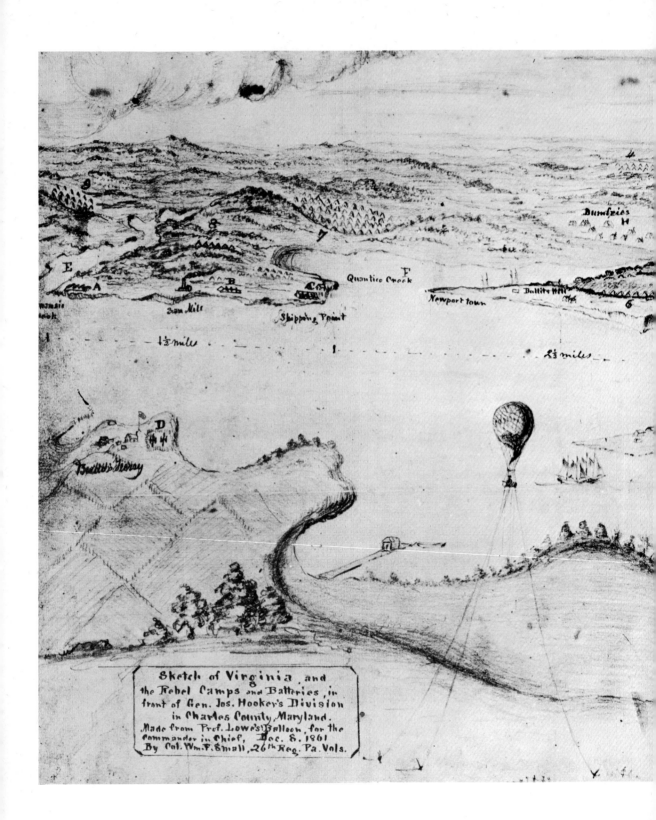

9

8

7

Dumfries H

E
A
B
Saw Mill
Co.
Shipping Point
Quantico Creek
Newport town
Bullits Hill
4

S

1½ mile

1

2½ miles

D

Bullits Battery

Sketch of Virginia, and
the Rebel Camps and Batteries, in
front of Gen. Jos. Hooker's Division
in Charles County Maryland.
Made from Prof. Lowe's Balloon, for the
Commander in Chief, Dec. 8, 1861
By Col. Wm. F. Small, 26th Reg. Pa. Vols.

Powell's Creek

Freestone Point

Cock-pit Point

2 miles

Stump Neck

Chickamoxen River

5 The forerunner of modern air maps. A sketch of Virginia during the American Civil War made from Thaddeus Lowe's balloon in December, 1861. (Photo: Smithsonian Institution, Washington).

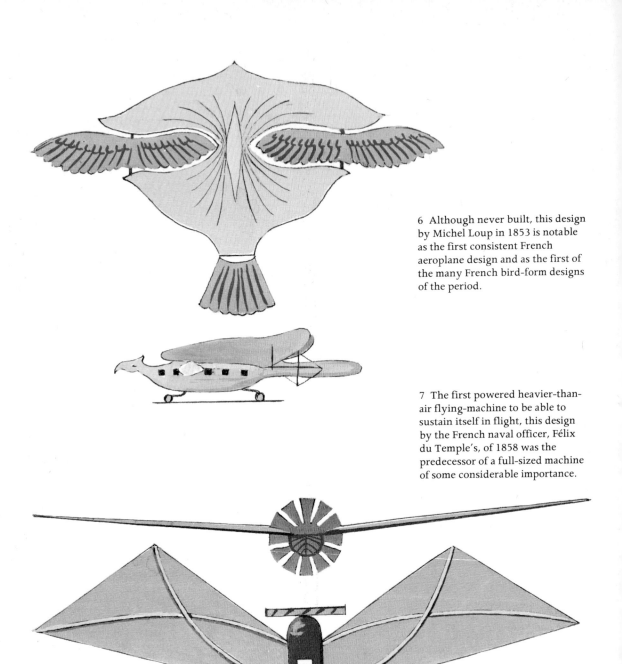

6 Although never built, this design by Michel Loup in 1853 is notable as the first consistent French aeroplane design and as the first of the many French bird-form designs of the period.

7 The first powered heavier-than-air flying-machine to be able to sustain itself in flight, this design by the French naval officer, Félix du Temple's, of 1858 was the predecessor of a full-sized machine of some considerable importance.

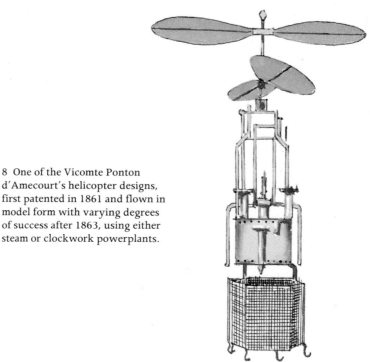

8 One of the Vicomte Ponton d'Amecourt's helicopter designs, first patented in 1861 and flown in model form with varying degrees of success after 1863, using either steam or clockwork powerplants.

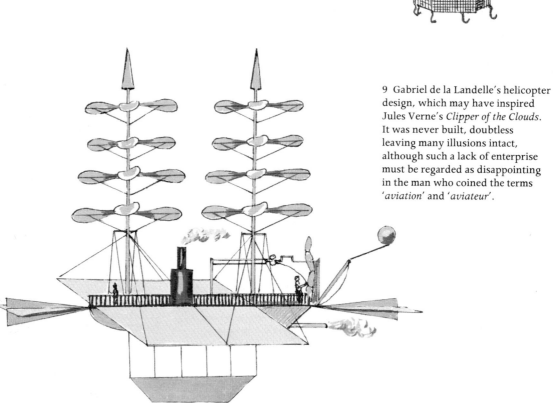

9 Gabriel de la Landelle's helicopter design, which may have inspired Jules Verne's *Clipper of the Clouds*. It was never built, doubtless leaving many illusions intact, although such a lack of enterprise must be regarded as disappointing in the man who coined the terms *'aviation'* and *'aviateur'*.

10 Not least amongst the French advocates of bird-form flying-machines during the 1850s and 1860s was the Count Ferdinand Charles Honoré Philippe d'Esterno (1806–83), whose designs, published in 1863, were intended to pay particular attention to the possibilities of soaring rather than gliding flight. This is typical of one of d'Esterno's designs, even to the point of not being built!

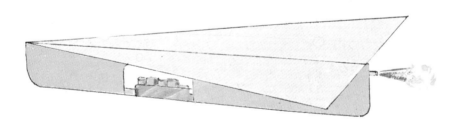

11 Not the forerunner of the paper dart aeroplane, but a futuristic British design for a rocket-powered aeroplane as early as 1867, by J.W.Butler and E.Edwards.

12 Probably the first photograph of a flying-machine, this is Jean Marie Le Bris's second glider in 1868. This was another of the bird-form designs, but at least Le Bris had the benefit of gliding trials with his first machine – if a broken leg can be counted as a benefit! (Photo: Musée de l'Air, Paris).

13 John Stringfellow's second design, if one excludes his work as a partner of Henson, which appeared at the first exhibition of the then Aeronautical Society in 1868. Unfortunately, this was probably his least successful work, aerodynamically. (Photo: Science Museum, London).

14 The engine for Stringfellow's 1868 design, which won a prize of £100 for the engine with the best power-weight ratio at the Aeronautical Society's exhibition. (Photo: Royal Aeronautical Society).

15 The first aeronautical exhibition
in the world, organised at the
Crystal Palace in London by the
Aeronautical Society, later Royal
Aeronautical Society.
Stringfellow's model can be seen
suspended from a launching wire,
while behind the first group of
visitors can be seen Kaufman's
model steam-powered ornithopter
with its locomotive-type chimney.
(Photo: Royal Aeronautical Society).

Chapter 5

THE PACE QUICKENS

Experiments in propulsion, successful models, first take-offs,
Pénaud, Du Temple, Brown, Moy, Pettigrew, Marey, Tatin.

*'Allow me, however, to express my
conviction that, in the future more or
less distant, science will create a light
motor that will enable us to solve the
problem of aviation.'*

ALPHONSE PÉNAUD, 1876

A science which had inspired half as much enthusiasm as aeronautics could not have remained in a state of hesitation and relative stagnation for long, and the poor progress of the middle years of the nineteenth century failed to blight the achievements of the final quarter. The advocates of heavier-than-air flight were once again throwing up from their midst men of vision and achievement, ensuring a quickening of the pace of development and an increasing conviction that problems existed to be solved, rather than to act as barriers to progress.

This is not to say that doubts did not persist amongst the onlookers, indeed it is well known that the doubters persisted until even after the first aeroplane flights. The real point, however, must be that those working towards heavier-than-air flight were increasingly aware that they were not on their own; work was being more widely publicised through the various aeronautical societies, and recognition, if still difficult, was easier and quicker than it had been.

The time was right, too. After all, was this not the age of man's supremacy over his environment? The period of change and progress which had seen, within so few years, the steam engine alter the habits and patterns of centuries? If, in retrospect, one were to muse over the fact that a future rival and usurper to the steam engine was coming close to reality with the development of the electric motor, it could also be taken for granted that this further evidence of change would be seen by many as a source for encouragement. In fact, one should be thinking in terms of rivals and usurpers for the steam engine, and the need for these has already been established.

On a more humble level, but hardly down-to-earth, balloons continued to play an important role in events at this time. The Franco-Prussian War resulted in the Siege of Paris during 1870–71. In an attempt to take passengers and mail out of the beleaguered city, a balloon factory was established in the Gare du Nord and sixty-eight balloons constructed. Thirty-six of the balloons landed safely in French territory after leaving Paris, while the rest either landed in enemy-held territory, or drifted to other countries, including one which strayed as far as Norway! All but one of the balloons were manned. The success rate might appear to be low, but it must be remembered that we are thinking about balloons, not steerable airships.

Even while at war, the French did not neglect the progress of aeronautics, or perhaps it was because of the war that they felt that they could not neglect it.

Gustave Trouvé built a model ornithopter in 1870, which was powered by twelve blank revolver cartridges fired automatically. This machine succeeded in flying for two hundred feet after a mid-air launch from a balloon; no doubt the flight was accompanied by spectacular, if not alarming, sound effects, and perhaps it was just as well that Trouvé abandoned plans for a man-carrying version. Although this was probably the first ornithopter to fly, the claim to flight is not a scientific one since the machine did not take-off under its own power.

Without a doubt, the outstanding figure of the decade was Alphonse Pénaud (1850–80) who, denied a career in the French Navy due to ill-health, devoted the last ten years of his life, so tragically short, to aeronautics. His first achievement was a twisted rubber motor for models, and although Pénaud did not pioneer this form of propulsion, which was the brainchild of Sir George Cayley, he did bring it to public attention – in itself no mean feat! The rubber motor was first applied by Pénaud to a successful contra-rotating helicopter design in 1870.

Pénaud's first real contribution to the technological development of aeronautics was his model 'planophore' of 1871, which was the first inherently stable monoplane design, possessing a mainplane in front of the tailplane, and a rubber-powered pusher-propeller. The mainplane was slightly tapered, with some dihedral for stability. A successful demonstration took place on 18th August, 1871, before prominent members of the Société d'Aviation, with the 'planophore' flying for 131 feet.

To an extent the 'planophore' overlapped, unwittingly, some of Sir George Cayley's early work, although the model was also the ancestor of every flying aeroplane toy. Pénaud was later to become one of the leading admirers of Cayley's work, and did as much as anyone to ensure that due credit and attention were given to the Englishman's achievements.

After this, twisted rubber-powered models became increasingly common. One such model came from Jobert, who built a two-wing rubber-powered ornithopter in 1871, and then followed this with a four-wing model in 1872. Pénaud's own ornithopter model of 1874 was also rubber-powered, and enjoyed some success, as did one developed in 1875 by another prominent French aeronaut of the time, Victor Tatin (1843–1913), and a model ornithopter by Hereau de Villeneuve.

It should not be thought that the period was taken up with rubber-powered, or even by revolver cartridge-powered ornithopters. Developments were in fact wide-ranging, including the first wind tunnel, built in England by F. H. Wenham and John Browning in 1871. On the other hand, not so far removed from the Trouvé ornithopter, was the suggestion, also in 1871, by Pomés and De la Pauze of a gunpowder-powered helicopter which would also have a variable-pitch rotor. Fortunately, it was never built.

Prigent designed a tentative tandem-wing ornithopter monoplane in 1871, basing his design on the dragonfly, while Danjard also designed a tandem-wing ornithopter monoplane, but with the flappers fitted between the front and the back wings. More realistically, interest in gliding flight continued, with a primitive kite-glider tested in South Africa by I. G. Household in 1871; while two years later, in France, Charles Renard built and tested a multi-wing glider based on Wenham's designs. In Germany, Otto Lilienthal continued along his own particular path to fame, with an 'aeroplane-kite' of pleasing appearance. Linfield, in England, built a glider in the Wenham-Renard mould.

One of the highlights of the age must have been the long overdue test flight of Félix du Temple's full-sized flying-machine, powered by steam. A young sailor who had volunteered for the mission, but whose name is lost to history, drove the machine down-ramp to the first take-off by a full-sized, heavier-than-air powered flying-machine. This was in 1874. The achievement does not rank as the first flight by an aeroplane, although there were those who claimed it as such for many years afterwards. Prominent amongst the requirements for true flight by a heavier-than-air machine must be the ability to sustain flight after the momentum of the take-off run or launching is lost, and ideally the machine should be able to lift itself off the ground and land on a surface no lower than that from which it took off. It might seem to be a fine distinction, but there is a world of difference between true flight and a powered hop or leap; and the Du Temple machine merely hopped.

Less successful, to the point of being tragic, was the fate of the man-powered ornithopter designed and built by a Belgian cobbler, Vincent de Groof. In 1874, De Groof took his ornithopter to England to make its first flights. The first of these, under a balloon which ascended on 29th June, did not result in the release of the machine, but merely allowed De Groof to flap the wings and tail. The second, on 9th July, saw the ornithopter released from the balloon, but the air pressure on the huge wings and tail folded these back uncontrollably, and De Groof plunged to his death.

Although never built, a more prophetic and practical device was a helicopter designed by Achenbach in 1874, which featured additional propellers for propulsion, rather like a present day compound helicopter, and a small rotor to counter the rotation effects on the fuselage. This was to be powered by steam, while an earlier machine, built by Renoir in 1872, was pedal-powered.

The days of steam-propulsion were numbered, for in 1876 the German engineer, N. A. Otto, designed and built the world's first practical internal combustion engine to use liquid fuel. A gas-powered internal combustion engine had been tested four years before this by Henlein, with the novel but not entirely practical method of using the envelope's gas as fuel.

Pénaud had not retired from the scene, however. In 1876 he designed, with the help of his mechanic, Paul Gauchet, a twin-engined monoplane amphibian which in almost every detail was well ahead of its time. The Pénaud-Gauchet had contra-rotating propellers, mounted one in each wing to counter any directional stresses, elliptical wings with cambered surfaces, slight dihedral and incidence, a tailplane with a fixed fin and movable rudder, and elevators, with these surfaces moved by a single control in the glass domed and well instrumented cockpit, and, finally, a retractable undercarriage with shock absorbers and tail-skid. The planned airspeed was to be in the region of 60 mph.

In spite of the undoubted brilliance of the design, its success had it been built is not beyond question. Apart from the problems of finding a suitable powerplant, and any questions about the structure – although this seemed to have been well enough conceived – the real doubt must be whether the design could be controlled properly. This was a feature of Pénaud's work. He went to considerable lengths to build stability into his designs, but the greater the stability of an aeroplane, the greater are the problems of control since aircraft become progressively less responsive to the controls as stability is increased. Obviously, Pénaud's theories about stability produced some fine models, but there is no point in building a full-sized aeroplane unless the pilot is to be allowed some control over it.

Pénaud committed suicide in 1880, depressed by his own poor health and by the scathing, and often unjustified, criticisms of his work from certain quarters. That his life was so fruitful in such a short span must, of course, encourage speculation about what might have been had he lived longer.

Not all of the major strides forward should be credited to the French at this time. It was an Englishman, D.S. Brown, who first conducted a series of scientific tests into the problems of longitudinal stability, using a number of tandem-wing monoplane models known, not incorrectly but nevertheless confusingly in the light of subsequent aeronautical vocabulary, as aero bi-planes. A full account of the tests, with illustrations, appeared in the 1874 report of the Royal Aeronautical Society, arousing the interests of an American, Samuel P. Langley, who was later to become an important figure in aeronautics. Langley visited England to study Brown's findings further.

Another Englishman, Thomas Moy, built a large tandem-wing monoplane model, the 'Aerial Steamer', in 1874, which was, as the name suggests, steam-powered. A three horsepower engine was used, driving two large six-bladed, fan-type, airscrews which were placed on either side of the fuselage behind the fore-plane. Tethered tests in 1875 at the Crystal Palace resulted in the 'Aerial Steamer' becoming airborne and reaching the staggering altitude of six inches. Subsequently damaged during a storm, it was rebuilt, but faded from history anyway. Moy was later to build a very small rubber-powered model in which he made the fore-plane markedly larger than the tailplane. This was tested successfully in 1879.

Another advocate of the rubber-powered tandem-wing monoplane was the Austrian, W. Kress, who built such a model in 1877.

Studies of the characteristics of bird flight were not neglected. An Englishman, Professor J.B. Pettigrew, published his *Animal Locomotion* in 1873, which made the point that the tips of a bird's wing fulfilled an airscrew function. That same year saw publication of *La Machine Animale* by a French photographer, E.J. Marey, who was the first to produce a series of rapid sequence photographs of birds in flight. Marey was later to produce photographs showing the behaviour of an airstream passing over an aerofoil in a wind tunnel, using smoke to illustrate the effect; this was modern thinking indeed!

The originator of one of the early jet designs, De Louvrie, proposed an ornithopter in 1877, although the 'Anthropornis', as it was called, was intended to be powered by a combined spring and petroleum motor mechanism.

Pettigrew's work inspired a design by F.W. Brearey, then Secretary of the Royal Aeronautical Society, for a 'wave action aeroplane', which appeared in 1879, using rubber propulsion and reinforced fabric flappers, and making a tentative flight.

The oldest surviving man-carrying flying-machine comes from this period. This is the glider designed and built by Biot, and in which he made a few very short glides in 1879. It can be seen at the Musée de l'Air in Paris.

A compressed air motor was used for the first time in 1879 by Victor Tatin, in a monoplane model with twin tractor propellers, a tricycle undercarriage, and the compressed air contained within the cylindrical fuselage. The Tatin model flew, tethered to a pole, for fifteen metres, or about fifty feet. This was more successful than a helicopter design by another Frenchman, P. Castel. When built, the helicopter, with no less than eight contra-rotating rotors, was supplied with compressed air through a tube running from the ground. An attempted test flight merely resulted in the apparatus lifting itself off the ground and crashing into a wall.

It would be fair to say that the helicopter designers, so busily active at this time, proposed, if they did not actually test, every known means of propulsion, and some as yet unknown. Emmanuel Dieuaide emerged in 1877 with a large steam-powered helicopter using contra-rotating rotors, and the limiting feature of steam supply through a tube from a ground-based boiler. A novel way of eliminating the weight of the fuel in a steam-powered design also occurred to the Italian, Enrico Forlanini, during that same year. The Forlanini method was to pre-heat the boiler, and then attach it to the helicopter, leaving the steam to move through to the pistons. Tested on a model, an altitude of forty-two feet was obtained.

An unusual design by one Melikoff, still in 1877, was for a helicopter with a screw-shaped rotor, which was intended to screw itself into the air, and return to earth by parachute. More interesting, the powerplant was to be a 'gas turbine' engine; in fact an early 'Wankel-type' design, but with eight chambers instead of the Wankel engine's three.

Hardly even deserving the description of models, but rather more like toys, were the rubber-powered contra-rotating helicopters built by Dandrieux in 1878 and 1879. These would climb into the air and then glide back to the ground using a butterfly-wing attached beneath the rotors. Ironically, the year in which Dandrieux started playing with his butterfly helicopters, was also the year in which the British army became interested in aeronautics, with the formation of a balloon unit within the Royal Engineers, based at Woolwich. The first balloon was actually the private property of an army officer, Captain J.L.B. Templer. This gave Britain the longest continuous history of military aeronautics.

The idea of flight was becoming firmly established in an ever greater number of minds; flight for peaceful and for warlike pursuits, ranging from mere toys through to ever more sophisticated, and sometimes even promising, designs. No one really knows just how many of the simple toys inspired future genius, but it might be fair to say that some of the most worthwhile contributions to aeronautical development during this period must surely have been the simplest.

1 and 2 One of the first airmail letters, sent from Paris to England by balloon during the Franco-Prussian War when the city was besieged. This was hardly a sure way of getting the mails through, with only 36 of the 68 balloons sent out of Paris managing to land in French-held territory. Indeed, the letter starts by expressing doubts about the fate of some earlier balloon mail letters. (Photo: Crown Copyright, Science Museum, London). ▶

Paris, le 16 Nov 1870

My dearest Nenn,

I wrote to Papa on the 8th for his birthday and to Willie on the 9th. I've just heard that two Balloons were taken by the Prussians last week so much I fear both my letters are lost, however we must expect that in such times as these, I shall be thankful if some of our letters reach you & C if I could only get one from you but I must wait & hope on, provisions are getting so scarce & are such a price that I think it cannot last much longer. I heard of a person yesterday who had just given 150fs for a hare which only weighed 10th, I've been asked 200fs for one but that was much larger, happily we don't want to buy yet — having still

two un... & plenty of other things — I wonder what sort of a dinner we shall have?!! I'm getting so anxious about you all I cannot sleep or enjoy anything, it is over two months now of which may not have happened in that time, then there is poor Willie may have wanted a little help it is very hard just as he is beginning business &c so lonely — Have you written to my poor little Emily? how I wish we had not sent her away, she would have been just as well with us if I had only known, but I am much better off than some I know who sent their children to the seaside with only a servant and now ... doubt & cannot know if they are still there or if they have any money to go on with, I don't really know what I should do under such circumstances but we have the comfort of knowing that our dear little Emily is in good

hands and has every thing she wants — A great many English get leave to leave Paris and we hear were robbed of every thing beyond the Prussian lines, how glad I am we were not among the number, but I expect you know in fact we get no news from the outside here & are obliged to wait the issue of events in the dark as it were, beyond this we go on just as if nothing was the matter & as a proof of this I must tell you that yesterday we bought a new carpet for our drawing room!! I'm so glad we took the English servant when we did for she is just what we wanted, Baby is so fond of her & she had him at night now until I get & she also makes us lots of nice English puddings &c..!! Henry has been confined to the house... days with a bad pain on his neck & tooth ache but he seems all right again now, Baby & myself are both quite well — Our united fond love to Papa, yourself & Willie believe me dear... Nenn

Your loving & affectionate... sister

Baby begins to talk... & has such funny little ways he is a real sunbeam in the house.

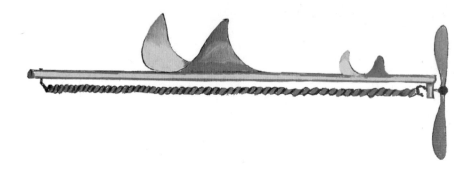

3 Pénaud's 'planophore' of 1871.
Not only was this the first
inherently stable powered
aeroplane, but also the forerunner
of the rubber-powered model
aeroplanes of today.

4 Only limited success was
achieved by this, Pénaud's rubber-
powered ornithopter model of
1874, which was only one of many
ornithopter designs using rubber
twisted for propulsion at this time.

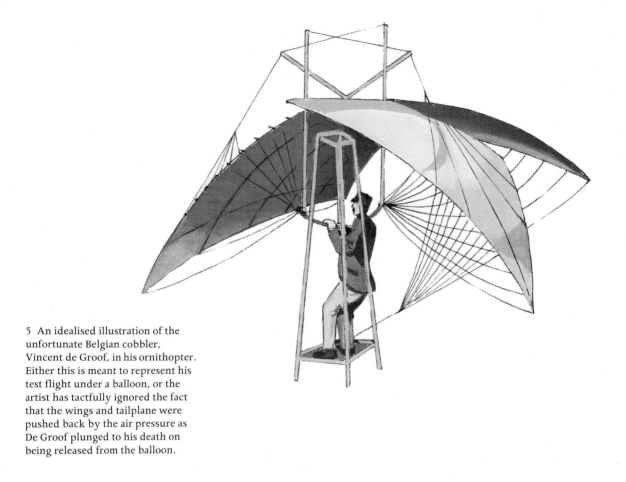

5 An idealised illustration of the unfortunate Belgian cobbler, Vincent de Groof, in his ornithopter. Either this is meant to represent his test flight under a balloon, or the artist has tactfully ignored the fact that the wings and tailplane were pushed back by the air pressure as De Groof plunged to his death on being released from the balloon.

6 Achenbach's hopeful helicopter design of 1874, which was never built.

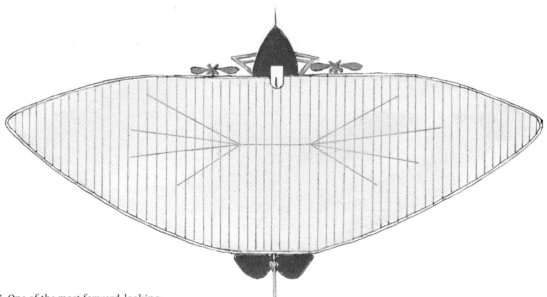

7 One of the most forward-looking aeroplane designs of the period before the first powered flight was this by Pénaud and his mechanic, Paul Gauchet, in 1876. The twin-engined monoplane amphibian incorporated many features which were not to become standard until the late 1930s, although unfortunately it was never built.

8 Thomas Moy's 'Aerial Steamer' of 1874, a large tandem-wing monoplane model which managed to reach the altitude of six inches on tethered trials in 1875.

9 Henri Giffard's large hydrogen balloon of 1878, which made a tethered ascent from the courtyard of the Tuilleries in Paris. (Photo: Science Museum, London). ▶

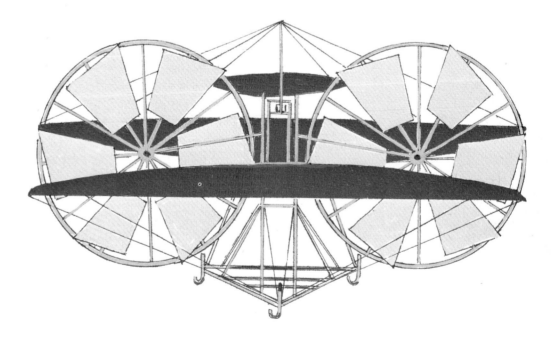

10 The first airmail stamp, issued for mail carried by the 'Buffalo' balloon at Nashville, Tennessee, in 1877. The stamp is pale blue in colour. (Photo: Science Museum, London).

11 Victor Tatin's model compressed air monoplane of 1879, which managed to fly for fifty feet while tethered to a post.

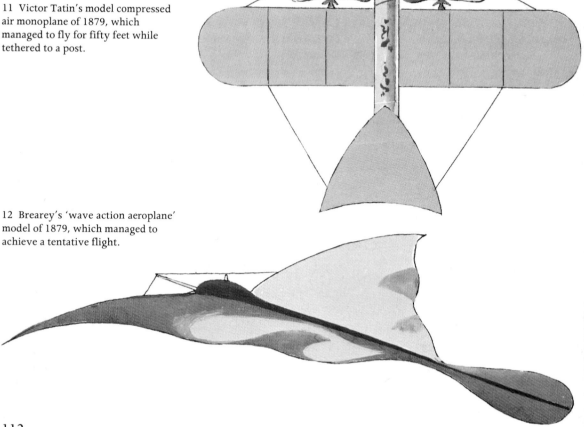

12 Brearey's 'wave action aeroplane' model of 1879, which managed to achieve a tentative flight.

Chapter 6

NEARLY, BUT NOT QUITE ...

Near practical dirigibles, powered hops, advances in propulsion, Tissandier brothers, Renard and Krebs, Mozhaiski, Goupil, Phillips, Hargrave, Ader, Maxim, Langley.

'But we must admit the possibility that continued investigation and experience will bring us ever nearer to that solemn moment, when the first man will rise from earth by means of wings, if only for a few seconds, and marks that historical moment which heralds the inauguration of a new era in our civilisation.'

OTTO LILIENTHAL, 1891

In contrast with the situation when Cayley died, the premature death of Pénaud was not followed by a slackening of the pace of aeronautical activity. This is an indication of just how far the science had advanced, for not only was Pénaud not alone at the time of his achievements, but other important figures crowd onto the stage after his departure. Indeed, aeronautical progress was by this time in the happy position of being unstoppable. It would be small exaggeration to suggest that the last twenty-five years before the Wright Brothers' epic flights of December, 1903, were to see a frenzy of activity as aeronauts vied with one another to be first. The scene was not so much that of a rehearsal for the great day, but more like a cattle stampede towards a much-needed waterhole!

Surprisingly, at a time when there was already such an accumulation of knowledge about flight, many seemed to still ignore all that had gone before them, and followed their own pet theories.

Almost as though summarising progress to-date, Dieuaide published, in 1880, two large wallcharts, 'Tableau d'Aviation' and 'Tableau d'Aerostation', which illustrated many of the designs which had been produced for both heavier-than-air and lighter-than-air craft.

Mouillard, of whom we have already heard, published his *Empire de l'Air* in 1881, which was later translated and published in the United States, and interested both Octave Chanute and the Wright Brothers. This was Mouillard's major contribution to knowledge of soaring flight, although he had never built a really successful glider himself, and his contribution to aeroplane control, his much-vaunted ailerons, were really air-brakes of a kind already proposed by others, including Pénaud, which assisted steering by creating drag.

In practical terms, the next real event in aeronautical development was the construction of an airship by the Frenchmen, Albert and Gaston Tissandier — two brothers who built a 92 foot long airship powered with a $1\frac{1}{2}$ hp Siemens electric motor. However, on a test flight which took place in a slight wind at Auteuil, in France, on 8th October, 1883, only minimal control could be exercised with such a small motor. A year later, Lieutenant Charles Renard and Captain A. C. Krebs built their dirigible, 'La France', which was tested with a considerable degree of success in 1885. The 165 foot long 'La France' managed to obtain a speed of 13 mph from its 9 hp Gramme electric motor, but in spite of this success, it was immediately obvious that the weight of the chromium-chloride batteries meant that any further development along these lines would be wasted.

Others were much encouraged by the work of the Tissandiers and of Renard and Krebs. In 1884, a Frenchman, Olivier, proposed a dirigible with large dihedral wings attached to the upper surface of the envelope and a horizontal tailplane. Later, one John Beuggar suggested an aerodynamically-shaped dirigible with twin airscrews, concluding that the balloon itself could not provide sufficient lifting power and therefore had to have propulsion in order to become airborne.

A timely reminder that the French and British aeronauts were not to have the field to themselves, or even to be allowed to share it merely with the Americans and the Germans, came at about this period from Russia. The first two important Russian aeronautical designs both appeared in 1881. N.I. Kibalchitch proposed a rocket-powered aircraft with a swivelling tailpipe for vertical take-off and for forward cruising flight. This highly futuristic design was never built. Also of some importance, was the design by an Imperial Russian Navy officer, Captain Alexander F. Mozhaiski, who produced and patented a design for a steam-powered monoplane with a single large tractor propeller and two smaller pusher propellers. Mozhaiski built his machine in 1883, and the following year it was driven down a ramp by I.N. Gulubev at Krasnage Selo, near St Petersburg, to a virtual repetition of Du Temple's achievement some ten years earlier. In fact, the Mozhaiski, using what must be recorded as the first British aero-engine export, managed to stay airborne for about one hundred feet before losing the momentum of the take-off run and returning to the ground. This event of Tsarist days has been claimed by Soviet Russia as the first aeroplane flight, which it was not!

Much interest must be attached to those designs which showed such considerable promise, but which, for some mysterious reason, were never taken to their logical conclusion by their inventor. One of these was a steam-powered monoplane with a single tractor propeller, designed by the Frenchman, M.A. Goupil, in 1883, which was never built. This was in spite of a full-sized test rig, without engine or propeller, managing to lift itself and two men in a 13 mph breeze! A later design by Goupil, in his book, *La Locomotion Aérienne*, published in 1884, incorporated fuselage-mounted elevons in an improved monoplane design which also displayed the designer's belief that the stability of a bird resulted from the curve of its stomach; although, interestingly, the movable tailplane did not incorporate a rudder.

An American contemporary of Goupil and Mozhaiski was one John J. Montgomery, who built his first monoplane glider in 1883. This crashed on take-off, and a second glider in 1885, and a third in 1886, also proved to be failures. A number of devices were fitted to the Montgomery gliders to assist with control in flight, but no real significance can be attached to Montgomery's work even though this came on the eve of significant strides forward by American aeronauts.

Nevertheless, two pioneers appear completely independently at this time, one an Englishman and the other an Australian, who were to prove themselves to be men of the stature of Cayley, Wenham and Pénaud. These were Horatio F. Phillips (1845–1926) and Lawrence Hargrave (1850–1915).

The Englishman, Horatio Phillips, registered his first patent for aerofoil design in 1884, and it was to be the first of several such patents during the years which followed. Phillips' patents were the result of several years of intensive research into almost every conceivable double-surface aerofoil section and angle of incidence, using a small wind tunnel in which the airflow was simulated by steam injection. As a result of this work, Phillips was able to prove his theory that, in a curved wing with a greater degree of curvature on the upper surface than on the lower, the greatest part of the lift is generated by the reduced pressure on the upper surface as the airflow travels over the upper surface at higher speed than over the lower surface. What had been a hunch for Cayley, refined into a shrewd suspicion by Wenham, became hard fact for Phillips, and for aircraft designers since. Phillips himself was later able to put his theories to work in a modest way.

Hargrave's contribution to aeronautics was considerable, but would have been greater still if he had lived in Europe or North America, instead of being cut off from the mainstream of activity by distance. It is wonderful to think that his efforts contributed in some way to the eventual ending of the isolation hitherto enjoyed, or suffered, by the antipodes.

The Australian's interest in aeronautics effectively dates from 1882, although he had in fact been a member of the Royal Society of New South Wales for some five years before this. His first paper dealing with aeronautics was read to the Society in 1885. Oddly for someone whose contribution to aerodynamics was eventually to be considerable, Hargrave started his experiments using rubber-powered ornithopter models. These had the feature of only having the leading edge of the flapper-wing rigid, thus gaining the maximum propulsive effect from the flexing action of the trailing edge; Hargrave's term for this action was 'troichoidal propulsion'.

Hargrave continued in this vein until 1889, when he contributed to one of the most significant steps forward in aerial propulsion by building the first rotary engine, although the Hargrave engine used compressed air, thus differing from the petrol rotary engine which was to prove so important during the first decade or so of aeroplane flight. A number of compressed air-powered ornithopter models were later built by Hargrave.

Ornithoptering still thrived, encouraged by the success of models and by greater knowledge of bird flight which together convinced many that this was a sure way to the skies. It should not be thought that this school of thought consisted of 'bird-men', since many large and sophisticated craft using this propulsive system were proposed, as we have already seen. Whether or not the advocates of ornithoptering flight were bird-brained is another question altogether, but even allowing for hindsight, advances in aerodynamic knowledge should have convinced them of the wisdom of an alternative course.

In England and in France at this time, ornithopterists included John K. Smythies with a steam-powered monoplane, and Pompein Piraud with a bat-wing ornithopter suspended beneath the balloon, 'L'Esperance', both in 1882. These were followed by William Cornelius in England, who, in 1884, built a manually-operated ornithopter, and in France by Pichancourt with a number of rubber-powered ornithopter models towards the end of the same decade.

On the other hand, interest in helicopters seemed to be at a low ebb, even if one counts the device built by a Frenchman, Hérard, in 1888–9, consisting of five frames of vertically mounted slats which rotated horizontally – to no good effect!

Strangely too, there was also a lull in glider design during the 1880s, even allowing for some of Lilienthal's early work at the end of the decade, of which more in a later chapter. Apart from Montgomery's unsuccessful efforts, a Monsieur de Sanderval in France built a tail-less monoplane glider which was towed by a cable, while one of his fellow countrymen, Arthur Battut, produced the first photographs to be taken from a heavier-than-air device late in 1888 – these were taken automatically by a camera carried in an unmanned-kite.

An event of real significance, however, was the construction by Gottlieb Daimler in Germany during 1884 of the first fast but light petrol engine. Karl Benz was but a year behind his fellow countryman in this, but it was a Daimler engine which was used by Wolfert in an airship in 1888, although the still low power output prevented this from being much of an advance on the Renard and Krebs dirigible.

Of virtually no immediate significance for aviation was the invention, also in 1884, of the steam turbine by the Englishman Charles Parsons. The long term interest in this invention is that it did at least help to prepare the way for the gas turbine of later years although, curiously, Parsons did design a helicopter model in 1893, which flew for some 300 feet, built not as an exercise in aeronautical achievement but merely to test a $\frac{1}{4}$ hp steam engine!

In spite of the tangible progress being made towards development of a suitable powerplant, the next serious attempt at heavier-than-air flight with a full-sized machine was to use a 20 hp steam engine. However, much about the

'Eole', Clément Ader's (1841–1925) flying-machine, was obsolescent, including the use of bat-wing construction with minimal control. A high-wing mono-plane with a single tractor propeller, the 'Eole', with its pilot sitting behind the boiler and either having to drive blind or peer around the fuselage, railway-style, was nevertheless destined for a significant place in aviation history. On 9th October, 1890, Ader managed to get the 'Eole' to take off under its own power and without any down-ramp run for assistance, for a hop of approxi-mately 163 feet at Armainvilliers, near Gretz. This was not the first flight, but it gave to France the distinction of the first heavier-than-air flying-machine to take-off entirely under its own power.

Obviously either very enlightened or capable of being fooled easily, the French Government of the day awarded Ader a generous grant for the construction of a flying-machine in 1892. The only real result was that Ader coined the French term for aeroplane, 'avion', by naming his second flying machine 'Avion II' and his third, 'Avion III'. Ader failed to complete the 'Avion II', and his 'Avion III' failed even to equal the performance of the 'Eole' when tested on 12th and 14th October, 1897. Basically, the 'Avion III' was an enlarged 'Eole', with the same bat-wing, although somewhat simplified, and two 20 hp steam-engines driving one tractor propeller, while the pilot still had to peer round the boiler. Doubtless, a contributory factor in the failure of the 'Avion III' was the decision to test the machine on a circular track, meaning that it was denied a good run into the wind.

If Ader had paid more attention to the known and published results of the work of the other pioneers, a different result might have ensued, for there is little doubt that he was a very good engineer and that the design of his steam engines was nothing short of brilliant. However, he has ruined his image for posterity by his claims, made in 1906, to have flown the 'Eole' for 330 feet in 1891, to have made a number of hops in the 'Avion III' on 12th October, 1897, and that he flew this machine for 1,000 feet on the second day of its trials. These claims were completely untrue, but delay by the French Ministry for War in publication of the official report until 1910 meant that they could not be completely refuted until that time.

John Stringfellow's son, F. J. Stringfellow, had also adhered to the steam engine when, in 1886, he had built a model biplane. This was the first biplane design to be built, but it was not successful, and had no influence.

The inventor of the Maxim machine gun in 1884, the American-born naturalised Briton, Sir Hiram S. Maxim (1840–1916) used much of the proceeds to further an interest in aeronautics. Like Ader, Maxim refused to pay much heed to developments elsewhere, although he was rather more practical and not so obviously dated in his thinking – one cannot say out-of-touch because both men were aware of the then current developments, but chose to ignore them for the most part.

Maxim started his experiments during the late 1880s, using a whirling arm and a wind tunnel to test aerofoils, experimenting with different propellers, and designing an efficient steam engine. After patenting a biplane design in 1891, Maxim completed construction of the machine in 1893; the completed machine was in effect a full-sized biplane test-rig, with monoplane elevators fore and aft, and designed to run along a length of tram track with upper guide-rails to prevent the apparatus from rising more than two feet into the air. On the third test run, at Baldwyns Park on 31st July, 1894, the machine lifted itself and the three man crew off the test track and fouled the guide-rails, after which Maxim shut-off steam.

It is perhaps unfortunate that Maxim chose not to pursue development of this design further, even though the control system was rudimentary. However, apart from allowing the test-rig to be used for a number of charity runs, suitably modified to prevent it from becoming airborne again, and from later attributing to it a greater influence on subsequent design than was in fact the case, he then opted out of aeroplane design for some sixteen years.

Also blessed with scant success at this time was the American, Samuel Pierpoint Langley (1834–1906). Starting in 1887, he conducted a number of whirling arm experiments before building some forty rubber-powered models, many of which were extensively modified during testing. These models were followed during 1892–4 by six steam-powered models, named, most inaccurately, 'Aerodromes', and numbered, equally strangely, from 0 to 5. The 'Aerodromes' at this time were unsuccessful, suffering from a lack of stability and wing distortion while in flight, in addition to problems with the launching mechanism, which was installed on the flat roof of a houseboat moored on the Potomac River.

Although Langley was to remain prominent in aeronautical development for some time, success at this particular stage was reserved for the Englishman, Horatio Phillips, who had taken out further aerofoil patents in 1890 and 1891. He followed these with the construction of a test rig in 1893, the rig consisting of a multiplane, or venetian blind of aerofoils, with a small steam engine driving a single tractor propeller. Tethered trials followed on a circular track at Harrow, near London, in May, 1893, with the rig rising about three feet off the ground at 40 mph. A later rig also proved to be at least partially successful, but Phillips for some reason abandoned further work until after the Wright Brothers' flights of 1903.

The development of the petrol engine did not at this stage have any effect on the modellers' choice of steam. Victor Tatin built a large steam-powered model monoplane in 1890, with assistance from Charles Richet, which used two airscrews, one tractor and one pusher mounted respectively at the fore and aft ends of the fuselage. The Tatin-Richet first flew in the year of its construction, and, after modifications, again in 1896 and 1897. Another French design, by Graffigny in 1890, was also steam-powered and successful in model form, as was one by the German, Gustav Koch, in 1891.

At this juncture a number of futuristic designs were amongst the very small number of aeronautical designs to come from Switzerland. Carl Steiger-Kirchofer, in his book *Vogelflug und Flugmaschine*, in 1891, produced a design for a twin-engined monoplane with a 'T' tailplane, with a detail drawing of a glass-domed cockpit. The following year, he produced another design, this time for a single-engined monoplane with a pusher propeller and a glass nose, in which the pilot was to sit. By some coincidence, another Swiss, Arnold Boecklin, proposed another advanced design in 1894. A further streamlined aeroplane design came from the Russian, K.E. Ziolkowski, in his book, *Der Aeroplan, oder die vogelahnliche Flugmaschine*, published in 1894, and this consisted of a streamlined fuselage with a four-wheel undercarriage, arched wings and a single tractor propeller.

In the midst of this furious activity, it should not be forgotten that the United States Army had followed the British by forming a balloon section in 1892, this move being prompted by the Spanish-American War. The British Army had sent its balloons abroad for the first time in 1884, in a military expedition to Bechuanaland, followed by another jaunt to the Sudan in 1885. Balloons, kites and parachutes were not being neglected by any means, although much over-shadowed by the more exciting events which were following one another in rapid and seemingly endless succession at this time. Increasingly, it was a brave man who could afford to seriously doubt the possibilities of heavier-than-air flight – in contrast with the trend of previous years in which only those who could afford to ignore ridicule would dare profess optimism about flight.

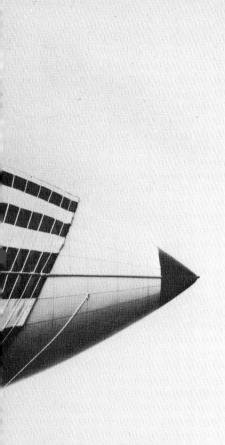

2 The brothers Albert and Gaston
Tissandier in the gondola of their
airship, 8th October, 1883. (Photo:
Science Museum, London).

1 A model of the airship built and
flown by Albert and Gaston
Tissandier in 1883. A $1\frac{1}{2}$ hp
Siemens electric motor, fuelled by
24 bichromate of potash cells,
provide sufficient power for only
minimal control. (Crown Copyright,
Science Museum, London).

3 Lawrence Hargrave (1850–1915), an Australian, made a number of important contributions towards the development of the science of aeronautics, including the invention of the rotary engine and of the box-kite, and a number of successful ornithopter models powered by compressed air. His attempts to build full-sized powered aeroplanes floundered, however. (Photo: Science Museum, London).

4 A model of the next airship to appear, 'La France', built by Captain A.C.Krebs and Lieutenant Charles Renard in 1883, and successfully tested in 1884. However, the weight of the batteries made it clear to the aeronauts of the time that no progress towards building feasible airships could be made using electric motors. (Crown Copyright, Science Museum, London).

5 A replica of Hargrave's compressed air-powered ornithopter model of 1888, which made a number of trial flights. (Crown Copyright, Science Museum, London).

1. Montgolfier fire-balloon.   2. Mrs. Sage, first English lady aeronaut.   3. Vincent Lunardi, first aerial traveller in England.   4. M. Charles, inventor of the gas balloon.   5. J. F. Blanchard, first crossed the Channel in a balloon.
10. Balloon mistaken for a monstrous animal by the villagers of Gonesse, near Paris.   11. Mr. Charles Green.   12. Green's night voyage to Nassau.   13. Car of Nadar's balloon, "Le Géant."   14. Mr. Cock

(18.) EXPERIMENTAL FLYING MACH

A. Julien's Aerostat. This machine, made in a model, 25 feet in length, moved by clockwork, succeeded in the experiment made at the Hippodrome at Paris.

B. November, 1851, Aerial scheme of Mr. Helle not yet tried; consisting of a combination of sails and screws, which were to have been moved by the strength of two men.

C. The Aerial ship l'Aigle, of Mr. Lennox. It proved a failure in the Champ de Mars, August, 1834.
D. Flying Balloon made by an engineer named Blainville.

It is not explained how these wings were to be used ; it gives the idea of weighting and lightening a ball with air by means of a pump.

ILLUSTRATIONS OF THE CENTENARY

st English aeronaut.   7. First ascent from Lyons, Jan. 19, 1784.   8. Mr. Henry Coxwell.   9. Perilous situation of Major Money. July 23, 178?.
gy_lliers.   16. Mr. James Glaisher, F.R.S.   17. Pilâtre de Rozier, first aeronaut, killed in 178?.

ed parachute by M. Henin.   This parachute was to slacken the ascent of the balloon,   H. Sir George Cayley's Navigable Balloon, 1816.
                                   and allow the action of the wind on the sails, thereby   I. Sanson's Aerostat, furnished with fins, made of
                                   guiding it at pleasure.   feathers; like Julien's, a motive power is required.

6 A century of ballooning, illustrations from the *Illustrated London News* of 26th January, 1884, showing seventeen of the most notable events in the development of aerostation between 1783 and 1883. (Photo: Library of Congress, Washington).

à monsieur Gaston Tissandier
en vous affectueux
Maurice Leloir 1887

7 Gaston Tissandier in 1887.
(Photo: Science Museum, London).
◀

8 F.J. Stringfellow's unexciting
biplane model of 1886 was the first
powered biplane, but does not
seem to have been successful and
was ignored by contemporary
aeronauts. F.J. Stringfellow was
John Stringfellow's son, and his
father's designs would seem to
have had some influence on the
biplane, even to the use of a
steam engine for power. (Photo:
Science Museum, London).

9 Clement Ader's steam-powered
and bat-wing monoplane, the
'Eole', in its hangar at
Armainvilliers in France. (Photo:
Musée de l'Air, Paris).

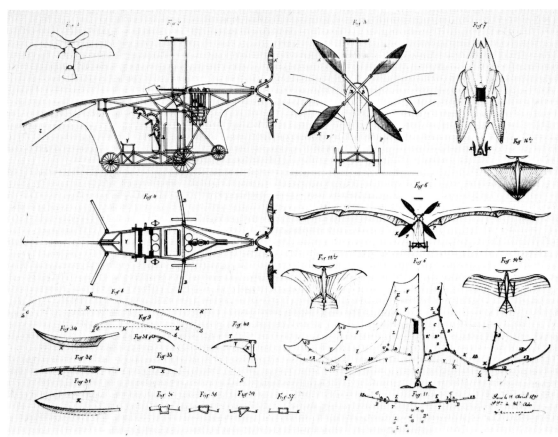

10 The first powered heavier-than-air flying-machine to take off under its own power and without any external assistance, the 'Eole' caught by the artist during its 163 foot hop at Armainvilliers on 9th October, 1890. (Photo: Musée de l'Air, Paris).

◀

12 A model of the 'Eole' cut away to show the steam engine, which probably had the highest power-to-weight ratio of any steam engine built for aeronautical purposes. However, the question of power-to-weight ratios for steam engines must be treated with some caution since much depends on whether or not the weight includes the boiler. (Crown Copyright, Science Museum, London).

11 Sectional diagram of the 'Eole'. (Photo: Musée de l'Air, Paris).

◀

13 Sir Hiram S. Maxim (1840–1916). Born in the United States but later becoming a naturalised Briton, he invented the Maxim machine gun in 1884 and later devoted some considerable effort towards aeronautics, even to employing Percy Pilcher as his assistant. (Photo: Science Museum, London).

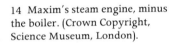

14 Maxim's steam engine, minus the boiler. (Crown Copyright, Science Museum, London).

15 Maxim's steam-powered test rig on its tramway track at Baldwyns Park in 1884. The track was 1,800 feet long, although on 31st July the rig lifted itself and its three man crew off the track after a 600 foot run. This is a view from the rear. (Photo: Science Museum, London).

16 A model of Phillips' aerofoil patent of 1893. (Crown Copyright, Science Museum, London).

17 Members of the Aeronautical Society on a visit to Baldwyns Park. A number of demonstrations of the test rig were given by Maxim, including some for charity, but usually with the outer wing panels removed to prevent any further attempts at flight. (Photo: Science Museum, London).

18 A model of Phillips's 'venetian blind' multiplane test rig, which undertook tethered trials on a circular track at Harrow in 1893, rising three feet off the ground at 40 mph in May of that year. The propeller is in front of the aerofoils. (Crown Copyright, Science Museum, London).

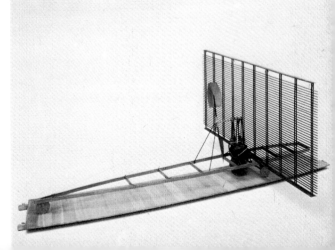

Chapter 7

HOME FOR CHRISTMAS

First practical airships, gliding flights, first aeroplane flights, Lilienthal, Pilcher, Hargrave, Chanute, Lebaudys, Wrights.

'Success four flights thursday morning all against twentyone mile wind started from Level with engine power alone average speed through air thirtyone miles longest 59 seconds inform Press home Christmas.'

ORVILLE WRIGHT, 1903

The story of man's early days in the air is full of blind alleys and the pioneers were continually being sidetracked or even, in some notable instances, effectively misleading themselves by a failure to take full note of the experiences of others. Tower jumpers and, to a lesser extent, ornithopterists, were at best misguided dreamers, and at worst the victims of their own nightmarish adventures. In some ways, the balloonists also only contributed indirectly to the advance of flight, since we now know that only the speed and the control possible with heavier-than-air aircraft makes the modern concept of aeronautics possible. Perhaps a little more credit can be given to the airship pioneers. However, the real trail-blazers for the aeroplane were the glider enthusiasts, simply because the fundamentals of aerodynamics apply both to the glider and the aeroplane, and a successful glider design is well on the way towards an aeroplane, basic perhaps, but an aeroplane nevertheless.

Mediocrity stifles rather than stimulates. Nothing is more likely to produce a flow of bright ideas than that there should already be ideas, or theories, in circulation, to be developed or challenged. The pump has to be primed. With a few exceptions, progress is really made not when one man works alone, but when many vie with one another for the privilege of being the first to achieve a certain step forward. In some ways, the work of the Wright brothers can be argued as being the effect rather than the cause.

A member of the Prussian Army besieging Paris, and doubtless a witness of many of the balloon ascents from the city during that time, was a young German, Otto Lilienthal (1848–96). Lilienthal had already conducted a number of ornithoptering experiments by the onset of the war, but afterwards he abandoned these in favour of a close study of bird flight, eventually publishing his *Der Vogelflug als Grundlage de Fliegekunst* (*Bird Flight as the Basis of Aviation*) in 1889.

Success did not come easily to Lilienthal initially. His first two gliders, the tail-less No. 1 of 1889, and the No. 2 of 1890, both failed in tests at Berlin-Lichterfelde. Nevertheless, these two monoplane gliders set the pattern for the rest of Lilienthal's extensive glider production, with rounded wings and radiating spars, the pilot hanging from the machine by his shoulders, and control being effected by moving the centre of gravity, in this case by having the pilot swing his body in the desired direction.

Lilienthal was having other problems, apart from any of glider design. Much time and effort was devoted to casting around for a suitable site for his experiments. Eventually he built a conical artificial hill with a hangar built into the summit. The hill permitted a take-off regardless of wind direction, but before this other sites were tried, including a springboard and rooftops. One suspects that Lilienthal was, at heart, a tower jumper par excellence!

Success came gradually to Lilienthal as he produced one design after another. His No. 3 glider of 1891, with fixed tailplane and fin, and a wing area of more than one hundred square feet, made a number of short glides, while the No. 4 of the following year, with about fifty per cent greater wing area, was some slight improvement. The No. 5 also appeared in 1892, with more than 170 square feet of wing area and wings which were arched and cambered, and this could glide for up to 300 feet in a light breeze – sheer size dictated that such a large glider could not be used in high winds. This was in fact the start of a degree of specialisation, not unlike that to be found in the suit of sails for a yacht.

The first really successful glider by Lilienthal was his No. 6, of 1893. This had a wing area of about 150 square feet, rounded, cambered wings, and a tailplane which could move upwards freely, which was intended to prevent the glider from stalling when gusted to a halt. With a tedious logic, the next glider was the No. 7, with about 25 per cent more wing area than the No. 6, and was very much a fair weather glider. The first 'production' machine was the No. 8 of 1894.

It was in 1893 that Lilienthal first toyed with the prospect of building a powered glider, curiously numbered as No. 16. A firm believer in ornithopter-ing flight, Lilienthal fitted six movable slats to both wing-tips for propulsion. A 2 hp carbonic acid gas motor was fitted, and the machine was glided in 1894 with the motor fitted, although no powered flights seem to have been attempted.

Returning to pure gliding with his No. 9 in 1894, named for the first time 'Modell Stölln', Lilienthal, either by sheer coincidence or perhaps because of a premonition, fitted a shock-absorber or 'Prellbugel' to the nose. The No. 9 was an excellent machine, but the shock-absorber saved Lilienthal's life when the glider stalled while gliding from the Stöllner Hills. Far from being discouraged, Lilienthal produced his small wing area No. 10, or 'Stormflügel-modell', for use in high winds, that same year. He did, however, take care to fit the shock absorber to this and all subsequent designs. Obviously, 1894 was a vintage year for Lilienthal, who produced yet a third design, the No. 11 or 'Normal-Segelapparat' ('standard sailing machine', the first reference to a glider by the alternative title of sailplane), which, like the earlier No. 8, was a 'production' model. A generally reliable machine capable of glides of up to 1,200 feet, the No. 11 was the first Lilienthal design to have the fin and tail-plane together in the now conventional position – before this the fin had generally been placed forward of the tailplane by the German.

Undoubtedly, Lilienthal's most complicated glider design was his No. 12, completed in 1895. This incorporated his patented leading edge flaps, to help reduce the risk of a nose-dive, and steering air brakes, although the latter feature was soon abandoned.

It was not until 1895 that Lilienthal first turned his attention to the possibilities of the biplane, which he saw as providing the same wing area as on his monoplane designs, but without the control problems associated with an unwieldy mass of wing. Three biplanes were built by Lilienthal, two, Nos. 13 and 14, in 1895 and one, No. 15, in 1896, with some considerable success. At the same time, he considered more advanced methods of control than merely swinging the pilot's body around, including simple wing-warping or flexing, an all-moving fin and wing-tip steering air-brakes, and he was even working on an elevator design at the time of his death. Indeed, he was much pre-occupied during 1896 with the problems of control and of gliding in a circle, which he never achieved because he was unable to attain sufficient altitude to avoid crashing into his launching point on turning.

A second powered design, the No. 17, was built during 1895–6, with ornithoptering wing-tips driven by a 5 hp carbonic acid gas motor. This, and a new monoplane glider, No. 18, was completed but untested at his death.

The circumstances of Lilienthal's death were tragic. Gusted to a standstill while flying a No. 11 glider on 9th August, 1896, in generally favourable weather conditions, he attempted to dive in order to gain speed, but only succeeded in stalling and then the glider side-slipped into the ground. His back broken, Lilienthal lingered on through the following day, but died during the evening.

Lilienthal's designs had a strong influence on both his Scottish disciple, Percy Sinclair Pilcher (1867–99) and the Australian, Lawrence Hargrave, although Hargrave's first full-sized glider was effectively a marriage of Lilienthal's ideas and those of D. S. Brown, the advocate of the tandem-wing. Unfortunately, Hargrave's glider was destroyed by a gust of wind while being flown as a kite in June, 1894.

Hargrave's real and enduring contribution to the science of aerodynamics was the box-kite! Ludicrous though this may seem to sophisticated twentieth-century minds, the box-kite was a considerable step forward at the time, providing maximum lifting power with a very high degree of stability, indeed, on one occasion Hargrave himself was lifted sixteen feet off the ground by a train of four box-kites, which were being flown in a 20 mph wind. The box-kite was first flown during 1894, and it was Hargrave's intention that his first powered, full-sized design in 1895 should employ the box-kite configuration, but this was not in fact built because of the poor performance of the steam engine chosen as the powerplant. A similar fate awaited his second full-sized, powered design in 1896.

139

A visit to London in 1899 enabled Hargrave to present a paper to the Royal Aeronautical Society, with none other than Percy Pilcher in the chair at the meeting. He also gave the Society several of his box-kites, one of which was carried triumphantly away by Pilcher for tests. The London visit was a success, earning for the Australian the recognition which he so richly deserved, but had previously been denied.

Returning to Australia, Hargrave built his third design for a full-sized, powered flying-machine, completing this in 1902. But again, the engine proved to be a failure. The aeroplane had been a multiplane floatplane, and the single steam engine was to drive a tractor propeller. After attempting a petrol engine-powered ornithopter, Hargrave abandoned aeronautics after about 1906.

Man-lifting kites had appeared in practical form by this time, invented in 1894 by Captain B. F. S. Baden-Powell, brother of Lord Baden-Powell, who used trains of monoplane kites. In 1901, the American-born Samuel Franklin Cody (1861–1913) patented his Hargrave-based man-lifting box-kites, which were adopted by the British Army in 1906. Cody was drawn across the English Channel in a kite-boat in 1903.

Percy Pilcher left the Royal Navy in 1885 at the age of eighteen to study engineering, gaining his aeronautical knowledge in the main from Sir Hiram Maxim, for whom he worked for a period, and from Lilienthal, including a visit to Germany after he had built his first glider, the 'Bat', in 1895. Pilcher also purchased a glider from Lilienthal while in Germany, and on his return made some considerable changes to the 'Bat', including modifications to the tailplane and a reduction in the dihedral of the mainplane, so that this was eventually able to make some reasonable glides at Cardross, on the River Clyde. In fact, Pilcher's second glider, the 'Beetle', also built in 1895, was a failure, and the third, the large 'Gull', completed in 1896, enjoyed small success.

Success in gliding was finally achieved by Pilcher with his fourth design, a hang-glider like its predecessors. This was his famous 'Hawk', completed in 1896 at Eynsford in Kent, while he was working for Maxim. A feature of the 'Hawk' was a substantial undercarriage, and the glider, a monoplane, was usually launched by towing; the procedure being for Pilcher in the 'Hawk' to be on one hilltop, while the towing mechanism was placed on the top of a neighbouring hill. Many very good glides resulted from the 'Hawk' using this somewhat unusual towing method, and a modified version of the glider was patented in that same year by Pilcher as a powered glider, although never built, and probably this was through the lack of a suitable powerplant.

Hardly a prolific designer, Pilcher's next glider was a triplane, completed in 1899, although he had also worked on, and bench tested, a 4 hp engine of his own design by this time. The triplane was never to be tested. On 30th September, Pilcher arrived at Lord Braye's estate at Stanford Hall, Market Harborough, with the 'Hawk', the triplane and his Lilienthal glider, to make a number of demonstration glides. Bad weather prevented Pilcher from attempting to fly the triplane or the Lilienthal, but he made two flights with the rain sodden 'Hawk'. It was on the second of these that the weight of the water-logged structure proved to be too much, and the tail assembly snapped, leaving Pilcher to fall thirty feet to the ground, dying two days later from his injuries.

One of the most neglected of the pioneers in the period immediately before powered aeroplane flight became a reality was the American railway engineer, Octave Chanute (1832–1910). This is due in no small part to his being presented as the catalyst which spurred others to take an interest in aeronautics. While this is largely true, particularly in Europe where he rekindled interest in flight during the early years of the present century, it is not the complete picture of the man. The first real aeronautical historian, his book *Progress in Flying Machines* was more than an accurate historical summary, it was required reading for every aspiring aeronaut. From 1900 onwards, he was a close friend of the Wright brothers.

Although too old to fly himself, Chanute designed three hang gliders based on Lilienthal's work and possessing a considerable degree of inherent stability. The first two gliders were built in 1896, including a multiplane of eight wings, later reduced to four, which made more than three hundred short glides, and a triplane, later converted to a biplane, which influenced Wilbur and Orville Wright enormously. Little seems to have been achieved by the third design, tested in 1902 at the Wright brothers' camp near Kitty Hawk by Chanute's associate, Augustus Moore Herring, who was later to be associated with the arch-rival of the Wrights, Glenn Curtiss. Herring also conducted some obscure experiments on his own account with an 'improved' Lilienthal glider.

Another American who, at this time, was also largely concerned with encouraging others, was the millionaire industrialist, James Means (1853–1920). Means' career conformed to the standard pattern of study of bird flight, kite and glider design, and he in fact built many model gliders himself, but his main fame, like that of Chanute, lies in the collection of important aeronautical papers which he edited and published in his three *Aeronautical Annuals* of 1895–7.

The aviators were not allowed to dominate the aeronautical scene, even during this eventful period. Balloons were being used for high altitude research, and in 1897 Salomon Andrée attempted to fly across the North Pole in a balloon, but died tragically after the balloon was brought down by the weight of the frost on the envelope. In Britain, the Aero Club, later the Royal Aero Club, was formed in 1901, and at this time its interests were very much tied up with ballooning.

Although he was later to be a leading figure in Europe's first aeroplane flights, a young Brazilian, Alberto Santos-Dumont did much to promote the cause of the dirigible at the turn of the century. His first airship was built in 1898, and a succession of small, almost baby, airships followed, culminating in his famous No. VI, with which he circled the Eiffel Tower on 19th October, 1901, travelling from St Cloud and back in $29\frac{1}{2}$ minutes. Essentially, the No. VI was a non-rigid airship depending on gas pressure for its shape, and power came from a 12 hp car engine, producing a speed of 15 mph. It would be fair to say that Santos-Dumont's airships were the first practical airships, although too small for commercial use.

A colourful figure, Santos-Dumont is generally claimed to have used his airships as others might have used a carriage or a motorcar, even to the point of landing in the Paris boulevards for coffee!

More usually recognised as the first practical airships in history, the German Count Ferdinand von Zeppelin was in fact still at the experimental stage during the early years of the twentieth century, although he was later to bring the airship to a fine art.

The French Lebaudy Brothers, Paul and Pierre, had the most un-aeronautical business of sugar refining. Yet, as early as 1896, their technical director, Julliot, had formed plans for airship production. With his employers, he later built the first Lebaudy airship, sometimes known as the 'Lebaudy I', or 'Jaune', because of its colour, which was completed in 1902. One hundred and eighty-three feet long, semi-rigid, with a keel but no internal bracing, the Lebaudy used a 40 hp Daimler petrol engine. Possibly its most notable journey was from Moissant to Paris on 12th November, 1903, covering the thirty-eight miles in 101 minutes. The airship was on display in Paris until 20th November, after which it returned to its home base at Chalais-Meudon, but was ripped open from nose to tail while coming in to land, although without injury to its crew. Subsequently rebuilt, 'Jaune' was also known afterwards as the 'Lebaudy II', while a succession of other airships from the same concern were built between 1903 and 1909, giving satisfactory service.

The first of Count Ferdinand von Zeppelin's airships, the LZ 1, ascended from a floating hangar on Lake Constance, near Friedrichshafen, on 2nd July, 1900, carrying a crew of five for a twenty minute flight. However, many years of experiment were to precede Von Zeppelin's later triumphs.

The enterprising American, Samuel Langley, had not been deterred by the

142

disappointing results of his early experiments. He rebuilt his 'Aerodrome No. 5' to a tandem-wing configuration, which he had discovered from a study of the work of, and a visit to, the Englishman, D. S. Brown. At the same time, 'Aerodrome No. 4' received a similar reconstruction, becoming 'No. 6'. These were Langley's first successful models, with the No. 5 flying for 3,300 feet on 6th May, 1896, and the No. 6 flying for $\frac{3}{4}$ mile on 28th November.

Two years later, the United States War Department, which seems to have shared the same kind of optimism as its French counterpart only a few years earlier, awarded Langley a $50,000 grant for the construction of a man-carrying aeroplane. Langley immediately contracted Stephen M. Balzer to build a 12 hp petrol engine of not more than 100 lbs in weight, leaving further development of the engine to his own associate, Charles Manly, who had to re-design the five cylinder Balzer rotary engine, which could only provide an output of 8 hp, into a radial engine. In the meantime, Langley built a $\frac{1}{4}$ scale model of his projected 'Aerodrome A', using a Manly-Balzer engine of 3·2 hp. However, the model failed to fly in a straight and level course during tests, and modifications took until August, 1903.

In spite of everything, Langley's confidence in his 'Aerodrome A' remained intact. When completed in 1903, the full-sized 'Aerodrome A' conformed with his now standard tandem-wing configuration, with the pilot sitting within the fuselage level with the front wing and in front of the engine, which drove two pusher propellers situated between the wings. Control of the aircraft was primitive, Langley simply hoped that it would have sufficient inherent stability to permit minimal adjustment in flight – and indeed there was little more than a combination of rudder control and engine power variation available to the pilot – the hapless Manly. Even though his launching system had discredited itself with models, Langley also arranged for the full-sized machine to be catapaulted off the Potomac River houseboat, with the one difference being that the mechanism was to be fitted under, rather than over, the aircraft.

On 7th October, 1903, the 'Aerodrome A' was launched from the houseboat, but fouled the launching mechanism and crashed into the river. A second attempt, on 8th December, was a repeat performance, even to giving Manly another unwanted ducking.

Langley's 'Aerodromes 5' and '6' had, however, inspired an Austrian, Wilhelm Kress, who built a full-sized float-plane in 1899, and this was similar to Langley's published designs for the 'Aerodrome A'. A heavy 30 hp Daimler petrol engine was used in the Kress, which did not even take-off, capsizing while taxying on the Tullnerbach Reservoir in October, 1901.

Even while others were indulging in often amateurish escapades, a more practical and cautious approach was being followed by two young Americans. The two Wright Brothers, Wilbur (1867–1912) and Orville (1871–1948) lived at Dayton, Ohio, where they owned a small bicycle manufacturing business. A casual childhood interest in flight appears to have taken second place to more mundane matters until 1896, when Wilbur's interest was re-awakened by the tragic death of Lilienthal. Three years on the usual study of bird flight followed, although Wilbur distinguished himself from the others who had gone before him in one vital aspect – the discovery of the need to effect lateral control and the invention of the Wright brothers' system of wing-warping, a 'helical-twisting of the wings', according to the brothers.

In May, 1899, Wilbur Wright wrote to the Smithsonian Institution in Washington:

I have been interested in the problem of mechanical and human flight ever since as a boy I constructed a number of bats of various sizes after the style of Cayley's and Pénaud's machines. My observations since have only convinced me more firmly that human flight is possible and practicable. It is only a question of knowledge and skill just as in all acrobatic feats. Birds are the most perfectly trained gymnasts in the world and are specially well fitted for their work, and it may be that man will never equal them, but no one who has watched a bird chasing an insect or another bird can doubt that feats are performed which required three or four times the effort required in ordinary flight. I believe that simple flight at least is possible to man and that the experiments and investigations of a large number of independent workers will result in the accumulation of information and knowledge and skill which will finally lead to accomplished flight.

The works on the subject to which I have had access are Marey's and Jamieson's books published by Appleton's and various magazine and encyclopaedic articles. I am about to begin a systematic study of the subject in preparation for practical work to which I expect to devote what time I can spare from my regular business. I wish to obtain such papers as the Smithsonian Institution has published on this subject, and if possible a list of other works in print in the English language. I am an enthusiast, but not a crank in the sense that I have some pet theories as to the proper construction of a flying machine. I wish to avail myself of all that is already known and then if possible add my mite to help on the future worker who will attain final success. I do not know the terms on which you send out your publications but if you will inform me of the cost I will remit the price. (*The Papers of Wilbur and Orville Wright*, Vol. 1, edited by Marvin W. McFarland, published by McGraw-Hill Book Company, Inc. 1953).

The list was duly provided, and one of the books mentioned, Chanute's *Progress in Flying Machines* (1894) was to prove itself invaluable to the brothers, inspiring Orville as well as Wilbur with the urge to fly.

The Wright brothers then plunged headlong into a programme of aeronautical development which would have done credit to many a corporation or research establishment, but which was solely the work of two young men, with the friendly advice of Octave Chanute and the meagre resources of their own business interests. Their first design, a biplane glider model, was completed in August, 1899, and then flown successfully as a kite to help the brothers prove their wing-warping theories.

One of the first results of their early researches and experiments was the clarification of two schools of thought on aircraft control: the inherently stable school, with minimal control; or the unstable school, which required continuous corrective effort from the pilot, although this enabled course and climb changes to be made easily. The view of the former school tended to suffer from an inability to appreciate that an aircraft has to move in three dimensions to be able to operate successfully. It is also difficult, as we have already noted, to control a stable aeroplane successfully, since the stability itself has first to be fought. Not surprisingly, the Wright brothers placed themselves firmly with those who favoured an inherently unstable design. It was Percy Pilcher, however, who discovered that excessive dihedral, which provided stability in normal flight, could also produce instability in a cross wind.

This was all done very quickly, the first full-sized glider to be built by the Wrights, their No. 1 of 1900, incorporated the principle of inherent instability and required the skill of the pilot to keep it aloft. Wing warping was included, and the Wrights also thought, at first, that this would steer the aircraft. Like all Wright designs, it was a biplane with the elevator forward of the mainplane, a layout which was thought to assist control. Only a few manned glides could be made with the glider during a spell at Kitty Hawk on the North Carolina coast during September; this was because of the almost complete absence of high winds, in spite of advice from the Washington Weather Bureau which led them to choose the site in the first place. However, many unmanned tethered glides were made, and the No. 1 was a success.

Experiments with the No. 1 had shown that a slight degree of dihedral contributed to stability and thus hindered control, so the No. 2 glider, completed in 1901, incorporated a slight degree of anhedral, while the brothers moved their camp from Kitty Hawk to the nearby Kill Devil Sands, where the rest of their gliding and their early aeroplane experiments were conducted. A first glide was made on 27th July, the glider being launched by one of the brothers and an assistant, while the other brother piloted, lying prone across the mainplane. Some changes to the wing structure were made to reduce the degree of camber, but in the end glides of up to 390 feet were being made in winds of up to 20 miles per hour.

So intense was the 1901–2 programme of study and re-evaluation, that work did not start on construction of the No. 3 glider until midsummer. This incorporated slight anhedral, an elevator forward of the mainplane, wing-warping, and a double fixed fin to provide stability while warping. Problems with drag while warping persisted, but the brothers soon discovered that the substitution of a single movable rudder for the fixed fins, and use of rudder and warping together, eliminated this. During the autumn of 1902, the No. 3 made no less than 1,000 perfectly controlled glides in winds of up to 35 mph and for distances of up to $622\frac{1}{2}$ feet, with a maximum duration of 20 seconds. The way was clear for an attempt at powered flight using a variation of the No. 3 glider design.

Such spectacular progress had not gone un-noticed, and indeed, reliable observers were wisely encouraged – wisely because at the time, while cynics persisted, experts were witnesses rather than observers in the modern sense.

In Europe, a French Army officer, Captain Ferdinand Ferber (1862–1909) had started building Lilienthal-type hang-gliders in 1899, although soon changing, on Chanute's advice, to Wright-type machines. He hastily built and tested a powered version of the Wright No. 3 in 1902, but without success.

At the same time, Karl Jatho, a German civil servant, built a 9 hp petrol engine-powered biplane, which, while possessing minimal control, made a powered leap of 60 feet in August, 1903, and one of 200 feet in the November.

These were the visible signs of rivalry in Europe to beat the Wright brothers into the air with powered flight, but it was very much a case of excited talk, and little action.

The sign of real genius and professionalism is the ability to make the difficult seem easy. The Wright brothers had this ability in no small measure, indeed, it is difficult not to be off-hand about their work. One is simply left to wonder how the bicycle kept them enthralled for so long!

Typical of the Wrights was their approach to the question of propulsion. Searching for a suitable engine, they discovered, as had others before them, that such a thing did not exist. They then set themselves the amazing task of designing and building a 12 hp water-cooled engine weighing only 200 lbs! At the same time, they studied propeller design, decided that no suitable design existed, so again, they designed and built a suitable propeller. To put at least the engine achievement into perspective, it must be remembered that only a handful of today's motor manufacturers existed at the time, and it was to be another seven years before the London General Omnibus Company was to consider that petrol engines were sufficiently reliable to allow full-scale replacement of horse buses.

Appropriately named the 'Flyer', later the 'Flyer I', the aircraft was built by the Wrights during the summer of 1903, and they travelled to the Kill Devil Hills in late September. The 'Flyer' differed from the No. 3 in having a twin movable rudder and biplane elevator while the engine drove two pusher-propellers, contra-rotating to avoid rotational stresses. The glider was modified to incorporate a 'Flyer' twin rudder so that the brothers could refresh their gliding skills before attempting powered flight. A single rail was laid, along which the 'Flyer' trundled on a launching trolley, requiring only one man to steady the machine on take-off.

It was not until 14th December that all seemed to be set fair for an attempt at flight. The toss of a coin decided that Wilbur should be first. The 'Flyer' made a perfect take-off run, rising from the rail only to stall and crash into the sand. Fortunately, little damage was done to the machine, or to Wilbur, who readily admitted to causing the accident.

The damage was quickly repaired, but flying was not possible until 17th December because of poor weather. Hastily summoning local witnesses and leaving a coastguard to press the shutter on a pre-set camera, the brothers prepared for a flight. At 10.35 am, with Orville piloting, the 'Flyer' trundled along the launching rail, took off into a 25 mph wind and flew an undulating course for 12 seconds, or 120 feet, at about 30 mph.

This was the first powered, controlled flight in history by a manned heavier-than-air flying-machine, and three more flights followed during that eventful day, Wilbur and Orville taking turns as pilot. The second flight covered 175 feet, the third, 200 feet, and the fourth, lasting 59 seconds, 852 feet, although, bearing in mind the wind strength, the last flight was for more than half a mile through the air.

The Wright brothers knew exactly what to do next, they returned home for Christmas!

1 (b) Lilienthal gliding, probably in one of his No. 11 'Normal-Segelapparat' gliders first built in 1894 and having a wing area of 140 square feet. This was one of his first designs to have tailplane and fin positioned together, rather than with the fin in front of the tailplane. This photograph actually dates from 1896, not long before his death while flying a No. 11, although the spectators would appear to have confidence in his abilities! (Photo: Musée de l'Air, Paris). ▶

2 Another illustration of Lilienthal gliding, again probably in a No. 11. (Photo: Musée de l'Air, Paris). ▶

1 (a) Otto Lilienthal (1848–96), the German pioneer who started his aeronautical experiments with trials using ornithopters, but turned his attentions to gliding after the Franco-Prussian War and produced the first pilot controlled gliders to become airborne. Appropriately enough for the man who once proclaimed that 'sacrifices must be made', he was killed in a gliding accident.

3 Lilienthal and No. 11 on the ground. Although he used a variety of take-off points, his favourite was from an artificial hill with built-in hangar. He does not seem ever to have taken off from level ground. (Photo: Musée de l'Air, Paris).

4 Lilienthal turned to the biplane glider in 1895 in an attempt to obtain high lift and wing area without the bulk of a single monoplane wing. He was surprised by the results, finding the new layout offered better performance in high winds and more positive control. This is his No. 13 biplane glider in 1896. (Photo: Musée de l'Air, Paris).

5 'One of the Last Flights of Otto Lilienthal' runs the original caption to this photograph of Lilienthal in his No. 13 biplane. (Photo: Science Museum, London). ▶

6 Percy Pilcher returned from his
visit to Otto Lilienthal in the
summer of 1895 with this No. 11
glider, having made some glides
under the German's tuition while
at Berlin. (Photo: Royal
Aeronautical Society).

7 A reproduction of one of
Lawrence Hargrave's compressed
air-powered ornithopter models;
this particular model originally
appeared in 1891 and made a
number of successful flights.
(Crown Copyright, Science
Museum, London). ▶

8 Another view of the preserved
No. 11, minus dummy pilot. (Photo:
Royal Aeronautical Society).

9 One of Hargrave's more sophisticated box-kites with its designer in 1898. Hargrave also intended to build box-kite based aircraft, but failed because of powerplant shortcomings. Voisin, in France during the early twentieth century, and also Alberto Santos-Dumont, did however build aircraft using box-kite techniques. (Photo: Science Museum, London).

10 Lawrence Hargrave about to fly one of his box-kites in Australia in 1894. As can be seen, his kites were rather larger than the popular toy which has resulted, and many of them needed two men to launch them (Hargrave is on the left of the photograph). (Photo: Science Museum, London).

11 Pilcher with his third glider, the 'Gull', which enjoyed scant success. The very large wing area must have given rise to some problems. (Photo: Science Museum, London).

12 Percy Pilcher (1867–99), a Scotsman who became interested in the possibilities of flight after leaving the Royal Navy. He benefited from contact with the German pioneer, Otto Lilienthal, and Sir Hiram Maxim, to the extent of following the German's belief that 'sacrifices must be made' and suffering fatal injuries in a gliding accident. (Photo: Science Museum, London).

13 Pilcher's fourth glider, the 'Hawk', shown here, was built in 1896 while Pilcher was working for Maxim. It was with the 'Hawk' that Pilcher finally achieved success in gliding, using the unusual combined towing and jumping launching method which he had devised himself. (Photo: Science Museum, London).

14 One of the rare photographs of Percy Pilcher in the air, in this case flying the 'Hawk', the undercarriage of which can be seen clearly. (Photo: Science Museum, London).

15 Pilcher's first glider design, the 'Bat' of 1895, with which he was able to make a number of moderately successful glides at Cardross, on the River Clyde, after modifications inspired by Lilienthal. (Photo: Science Museum, London).

◀

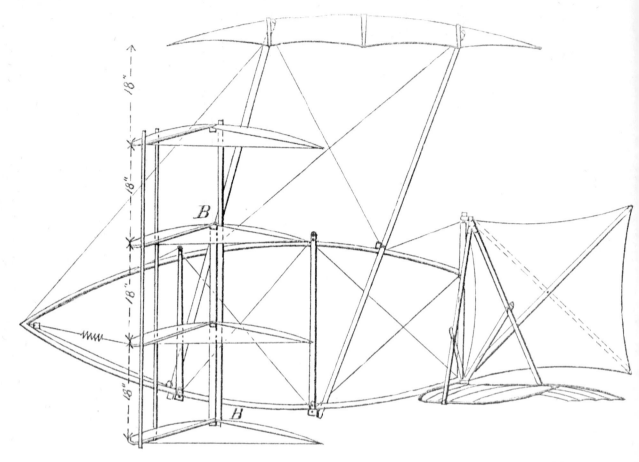

18"

18"

18"

18"

18"

B

B

16 A port side diagram of the
Chanute multiplane glider.

17 A front view of Octave
Chanute's multiplane hang-glider,
also built in 1896. Originally this
design was for eight wings, but
these were eventually reduced to
four, probably to reduce an
otherwise unwieldy weight. Some
300 short glides were achieved
with this multiplane. ▶ ▲

18 A plan view of the Chanute
multiplane, viewed from above.
▶

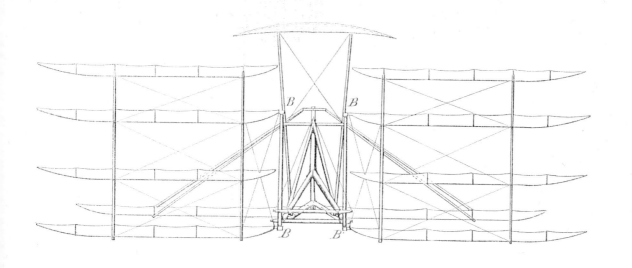

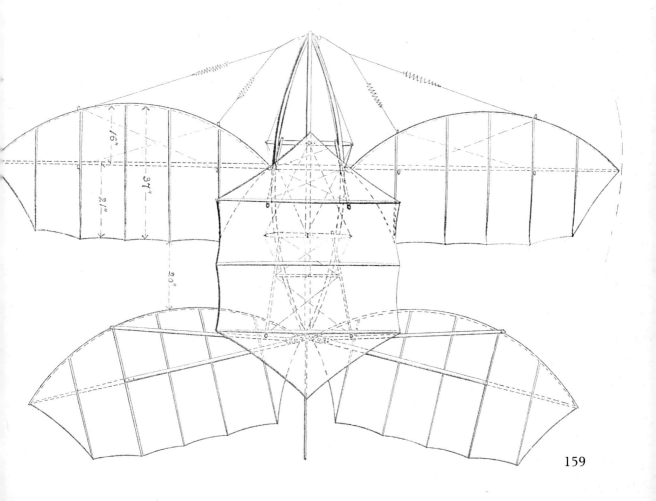

19 Alberto Santos-Dumont (1873–1932) was a wealthy Brazilian living in Paris. His distinguished aeronautical record included experiments with a successful series of small airships, followed by the first aeroplane flight in Europe in 1906. (Photo: Library of Congress, Washington).

20 A photograph of Alberto Santos-Dumont's No. 6 airship of 1901, after landing in the garden of Baron Rothschild in September; it is not recorded whether this was voluntary or not! The No. 6 circled the Eiffel Tower on 19th October, showing a considerable advance over earlier airship designs. (Photo: Bibliothèque Nationale, Paris).

21 A caricature of Alberto Santos-Dumont and his No. 6 dirigible; certainly, the Brazilian's activities almost gave the impression that he was a part of the airship. (Photo: Science Museum, London).

22 'My present aids understand my present airships' runs the original caption to this photograph of the engine for the Santos-Dumont No. 6. This seemingly condescending remark was in fact high praise indeed at a time when the advance of the automobile was seriously hampered by, amongst other factors, an almost complete absence of skilled mechanics. It was to take World War I to produce large numbers of men with an understanding of the internal combustion engine. The airship itself had been misunderstood at times, and these were still early days. (Photo: Science Museum, London).

23 The Lebaudy airships are generally credited with having been the first practical airships. The first one was completed in 1902, almost fifty years after the Giffard airship's voyage. This photograph shows the 'Lebaudy I' or 'Jaune', as it was often known because of its yellow colour, probably during its display in Paris between 12th and 20th November, 1903. (Photo: Bibliothèque Nationale, Paris).
◀

24 Other Lebaudy airships followed, and this photograph shows the 'Lebaudy IV', which has a family resemblance to the 'I'. (Photo: Science Museum, London).

25 A detail of Langley's 'Aerodrome A'. (Smithsonian Institution, Washington). ▶

26 With some stretching of the imagination, Langley's houseboat on the Potomac River could be considered the first aircraft carrier. His models, and eventually his 'Aerodrome A', were catapulted from the roof (in fact the first aircraft carrier for the United States Navy was named the USS Langley). This photograph shows the 'Aerodrome A' on the catapult prior to one of its unsuccessful launchings in late 1903. (Photo: Library of Congress, Washington).

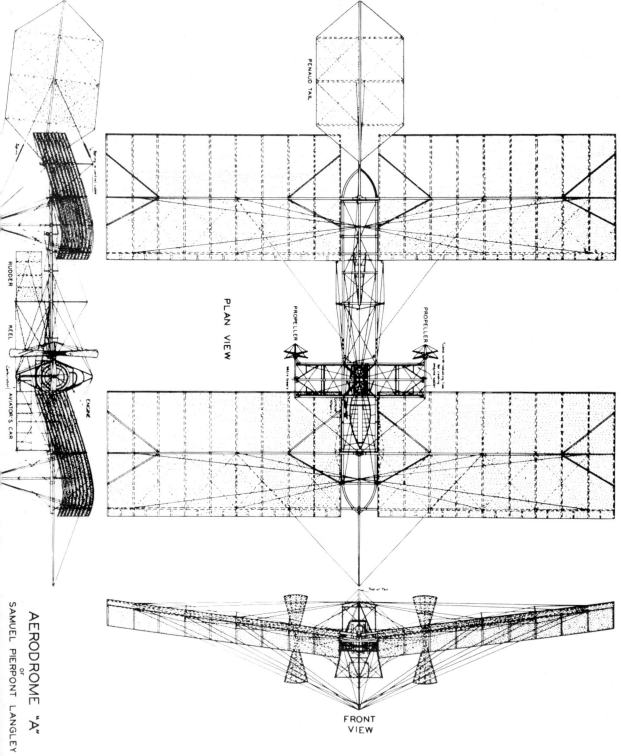

PLAN VIEW

PENAUD TAIL

PROPELLER

PROPELLER

RUDDER

KEEL

ENGINE

AVIATOR'S CAR

FRONT
VIEW

AERODROME "A"
OF
SAMUEL PIERPONT LANGLEY

27 Some years after the Wright
brothers' flights, their rival, Glenn
Curtiss, modified the 'Aerodrome A'
and made a flight in an attempt to
dispute some of the Wright patents.
This is the modified 'Aerodrome'
in flight. (Photo: Smithsonian
Institution, Washington).

28 Wilbur Wright (1867–1912), the elder of the Wright Brothers, was the first to take an active as opposed to a passive interest in the possibilities of aviation, and it was he who later made the series of flights in Europe which confirmed the leadership of the two brothers in the minds of their European rivals. (Photo: Science Museum, London).

29 Orville Wright (1871–1948), the younger brother, who nevertheless played his part in designing, building and flying the series of gliders and aeroplanes which established the reputation of the Wrights. His achievement in actually making the first aeroplane flight was the result of the Wrights' practice of taking the early flights in turns – Wilbur had failed to make the 'Flyer' fly during an attempt three days earlier, and had actually damaged the aircraft slightly. Orville was later to experience the first fatal accident during an aeroplane flight, when his passenger, Lieutenant Selfridge, of the US Army, was killed. (Photo: Science Museum, London).

30 The Wright 1901 glider, the No. 2, with Wilbur at the controls at the Kill Devil Sands, not far from their previous year's base at Kitty Hawk on the North Carolina coast. The slight anhedral introduced on this model can just be seen. (Photo: Science Museum, London).

31 The Wright No. 3 glider being launched on 10th October, 1902, at the Kill Devil Sands. Orville is at the controls. It can clearly be seen that this photograph shows the No. 3 in its later form, with a single movable rudder replacing the earlier fixed twin fins. (Photo: Science Museum, London).

32 Probably one of the greatest
disappointments in aeronautical
history, but fortunately only a
minor setback. Wilbur Wright at
the controls of the Wright 'Flyer'
after the minor accident on 14th
December, 1903. Too much elevator
as the machine took off caused it to
stall. (Photo: Science Museum,
London).

33 The first flight, 17th December, 1903, with Orville at the controls and Wilbur standing by, having steadied the aircraft during the take-off run. A camera had been mounted on a tripod before the attempt, pre-set and pointed towards the end of the launching rail, and a coastguard from the Kitty Hawk Coastguard Station told to press the shutter control at the appropriate moment. However, the brothers weren't sure whether or not they had a photographic record of their achievement until they developed the plate on their return to Dayton. (Photo: Smithsonian Institution, Washington).

34 The 'Flyer I', a view from the front. The twist of the drive chain to the port propeller to provide contra-rotation of the propellers can be seen clearly. (Photo: Science Museum, London).

35 A starboard side view of the 'Flyer I'. (Photo: Science Museum, London).

36 The first satisfactory powerplant in aeronautical history. The
Wright brothers had to build their
own engine to their own design
because of the absence of any
other lightweight engines of
sufficient horsepower. (Photo:
Science Museum, London).

37 The installation of the Wright engine on the 'Flyer I'. (Photo: Science Museum, London).

LA SORTIE DE L'OPÉRA EN L'AN 2000.

38 *'Les Encombrements'*, a cartoon
inspired by Santos-Dumont's
Eiffel Tower flight, foretelling an
obvious air traffic control problem.
(Photo: Science Museum, London).

39 *'La Sortie de l'Opéra en l'an
2000'*, another cartoon from the
turn of the century forecasting
aviation achievement. (Photo:
Science Museum, London).

Chapter 8

CONCLUSION

Practical aeroplanes, first flights in Europe, rocket and turbojet propulsion, helicopters.

'Anything that one man is capable of imagining, other men will be capable of making a reality.'

JULES VERNE

It took a little more than 120 years from the first manned balloon ascents to the first powered aeroplane flight, and in its own way, each of these events was the culmination of man's dreams over thousands, rather than hundreds, of years. The price had been immense, not so much in terms of finance, because even allowances for inflation cannot effectively disguise the fact that, in the early days, aviation started relatively cheaply, but in terms of human life.

The Wright brothers had still to build the first practical aeroplane after their flights in the 'Flyer', although they were much nearer to this end than the Tissandier brothers or Renard and Krebs had been to the practical airship after the conclusion of their experiments. Wilbur and Orville had still to achieve recognition for, in spite of photographic evidence, the results of their work, even when backed by witnesses, failed to be accepted by press, public or politicians. Perhaps the most bitter blow of all was to be the refusal by the United States War Department to recognise the achievement for some years, and this was the body which had so recklessly and willingly supported Langley after such minor achievements. Fortunately, the Wrights were not to be without recognition and fame in due course.

Improvement of the 'Flyer I' was an early task, and 1904 saw the first flights of the 'Flyer II', which was the first aeroplane to fly a full circle on 20th September, 1904. Of all the journals which might have carried reports of this event, it was left to an apiarists magazine, the January, 1905, edition of *Gleanings in Bee Culture*, whose editor, Amos I.Root, was a witness to what he immediately recognised as an occasion of historic importance. Wilbur was the pilot at the time, while an anxious Orville was busily occupied in trying to move Root out of the way for fear that he might be struck by the aircraft! Altitudes were in fact very low, and were to remain so for some years afterwards.

The first practical aeroplane, able to fly in circles, figures of eight, and to bank and turn, was the Wright 'Flyer III', first flown on 29th September, 1905. Tests with the aircraft during that autumn failed to make the authorities realise that the Wrights were offering a workable flying machine, not merely an idea, while a British Army order failed to materialise because of the natural reluctance of the brothers to demonstrate before purchase, for fear of imitations resulting. It was probably predictable that a period of more than two years should follow without further flights from the Wrights.

However, little happened during the period of grounding to topple Wilbur and Orville from their position of supremacy, and they returned to aviation in grand style, with a modified 'Flyer III' with which to make the first passenger-carrying flight, with Charles W.Furnas as Orville's passenger at the Kill Devil Hills on 14th May, 1908.

Events now started to move rapidly in the right direction. Wilbur arrived in France during the late summer, and proceeded to demonstrate the Wright 'A' biplane to a French audience which was at once astounded and humbled, realising the authenticity of the Wright brothers' claims and their superior control over their aircraft compared with the glorified hops of the Europeans. Meanwhile, Orville was demonstrating another Wright 'A' to the U.S. Army, although on one such flight tragedy struck, with an accident in which Orville was injured and his passenger, Lieutenant T. Selfridge, killed. The accident was caused by a propeller blade failure, in spite of Orville's near successful attempt at landing.

Europe had in the meantime left its own first aeroplane flights to the enterprising Brazilian, Alberto Santos-Dumont, who had achieved a tentative flight with his '14-bis' at Bagatelle, France, on 13th September, 1906, using a 24 hp Antionette engine in his biplane, which owed much to Hargrave's box-kite. Modified by the substitution of a 50 hp engine of the same brand, the '14-bis' made a further flight on 12th November.

Still, the Europeans could be excused for their seeming tardiness since it took until June, 1908, for another American to follow the Wrights into the air. Then Glenn Curtiss flew his Aircraft Experimental Association 'June Bug' on 20th of that month. On 4th July, Curtiss flew for almost a mile in the same aircraft, winning a 'Scientific American' prize for the first American to fly in public over a measured course.

There was a short period of further achievement for the Wrights, before the first serious challenges to their position emerged at the first international aviation meeting, at Reims in 1909.

The airship enjoyed a period of glory before World War I. There were passenger flights in Germany, followed by wartime reconnaissance and bombing duties, although during the post-war period strong competition from the flying-boat began to diminish the airship's reputation, a process which finally culminated in the Hindenburg disaster in 1937, although this was primarily due to the continued use of hydrogen because of an embargo on sales of the safer helium to Germany.

Rocket-powered aeroplanes did not appear until 1928, and then existed solely for experimental use until the Messerschmitt Me.162 Komet interceptor of World War II. The other thrust reaction engine, the turbojet, was developed in Germany by Von Ohain and in England by Whittle during the 1930s respectively, resulting in the Heinkel He.178 of 1939 and the Gloster-Whittle E.28/39 of 1941, while the first operational jets were the Messerschmitt Me.262 and Gloster Meteor fighters.

In spite of many experiments, it was not until Igor Sikorsky built his VS-300

180

in the United States in 1939 that the first practical helicopter appeared, although the German Focke-Achgelis of a few years earlier had helped to prepare the way, as had the gyroplanes of the Spaniard, De la Cierva, first flown during the mid-1920s.

If some of the seeds sown by the pioneers seemed to be long in bearing fruit, it must be remembered that for the most part the dreams of the most prophetic were exceeded – not the least being Cayley's prediction in 1809 that, '. . . we shall be able to transport ourselves and families, and their goods and chattels, more securely by air than by water, and with a velocity of from 20 to 100 miles per hour.'

One merely has to multiply Cayley's speeds by ten!

Chronological table of events

2200 B.C.	Chinese Emperor Shin reputed to have tower jumped.
1500 B.C.	Legend of Persian King Kai Kawus journeying to view the heavens.
c. 852 B.C.	Legend of English King, Bladud, killed while attempting flight.
c. 100 B.C.	Hero of Alexandria discovers propulsive effects of a jet of steam.
852 A.D.	Armen Firman tower jumps at Cordoba.
1020	Oliver, or Eilmer, of Malmesbury jumps from Malmesbury Abbey.
1200	Windmills in use in Europe.
c. 1250	Roger Bacon writes on prospect of flight.
1326	Walter de Milemete produces illustrations of a kite and of aerial warfare.
c. 1420	Joanes Fontana produces illustration of bird powered by 'rocket'.
1486	Leonardo da Vinci designs parachute, and starts ornithopter design.
1496	Senecio injured in tower jump.
1497	Leonardo da Vinci produces design for powered aeroplane.
1503	G. B. Danti injured while attempting flight.
1505	Leonardo da Vinci writes on bird flight.
1507	John Damian injured in a jump from Stirling Castle.
1536	Bolori killed while tower jumping.
1550	Bacon's work published.
1595	Fausto Veranzio publishes illustration of a parachute.
1638	First science fiction by English Bishops Godwin and Wilkins.
1648	Tito Burattini makes model 'flying dragon'.
1650	G. A. Borelli suggests that a man's arms alone are unable to produce sufficient strength for flight.
1655	Robert Hooke builds spring-powered model ornithopter.
c. 1658	Gaspar Schott writes on flight.
1659	Cyrano de Bergerac writes on travel to the moon (English translation).
1670	Father Francesco de Lana de Terzi publishes design of a flying ship, and describes aerial bombardment and assault.
1673	Bernoin dies attempting flight at Frankfurt.
1676	Francis Willughby suggests that man's legs are more comparable with a bird's wings than his arms.
1678	Besnier attempts flight at Sable.
c. 1680	Canon Oger tower jumps.
1680	Borelli publishes his work on the shortcomings of human muscle-power.
1709	Gusmão designs and tests a model of his 'Passarola'.
1716	Emmanuel Swedenborg publishes a flying-machine design.
1742	De Bacqueville attempts to fly across the Seine.

183

1749	Alexander Wilson experiments with a kite to record cloud temperature.
1752	Benjamin Franklin studies atmospheric electricity after flying a kite in a thunderstorm.
1754	Michael V. Lomonosov builds helicopter model, reputed to be capable of flight.
1764	Bauer designs fixed-wing flying-machine.
1766	Cavendish isolates hydrogen gas.
1768	A.J.P. Paucton proposes compound helicopter design.
1772	Canon Desforges designs and builds 'voiture volante' flying-machine.
1781	Blanchard produces design for man-powered flying-machine, which he later builds.
	Meerwein builds ornithopter-glider.
1782	Montgolfier brothers begin experiments with paper bags.
1783 *June 4th*	Model Montgolfier balloon ascent at Annonay.
September 19th	Farm animals ascend in Montgolfier balloon from Versailles.
October	Joseph Montgolfier proposes hot air reaction propulsion for balloons.
November 21st	De Rozier and D'Arlandes make first balloon voyage in a Montgolfière.
December 1st	Charles and Robert make first hydrogen balloon voyage.
1784	Launoy and Bienvenu produce model helicopter design.
	Renaux and Gérard produce ornithopter designs.
	Aries attempts to tower jump at Embrun.
September 15th	Lunardi makes first balloon voyage in Great Britain.
October 16th	Blanchard attempts to propel balloon with airscrew.
1785	Meusnier produces first airship design.
January 7th	Blanchard and Jeffries cross English Channel from England to France in a balloon.
June 15th	De Rozier and Romain killed in first serious balloon accident during Channel crossing attempt.
1794	First military use of balloon by the French Army at the Battle of Maubeuge.
1796	Cayley flies model helicopter.
1797 *October 22nd*	Garnerin makes first parachute descent, from a balloon.
1799	Cayley produces first design for a modern configuration aeroplane.
	Tipu Sultan's troops use artillery rockets against British Army in India.
1804	Cayley flies model glider.
1805	Congreve tests artillery rockets.

184

1807		Royal Navy use artillery rockets against Copenhagen.
1809		Degen makes leaps with his balloon-ornithopter.
		Cayley flies full-sized glider unmanned, and begins publication of his triple paper on aerodynamics.
1811		Tailor of Ulm attempts Degen-type ornithopters, without the balloon.
1816		Degen flies clockwork ornithopter model.
1818		De Lambertye designs ornithopter with helicopter ferries.
1822		Pocock flies man-lifting kite.
1827		Pocock's kite-drawn carriage tested successfully.
1830		Artingstall tests steam-powered ornithopter model.
1831		Walker published first tandem-wing designs.
1837	*July* 24th	Cocking killed during first test of Cayley's dihedral parachute.
1842		W.H. Phillips successfully tests steam-powered ornithopter model.
1843		Bourne designs and builds his first clockwork helicopter models.
	March	Henson's 'Aerial Steam Carriage' design published.
	April	Cayley's convertiplane biplane design published.
1847		Henson tests first powered aeroplane model, with little success.
1848		Stringfellow tests steam-powered aeroplane model.
1849		Cayley tests boy-carrying glider.
		Austrian unmanned hot-air balloons used to bomb Venice.
1852		Société Aérostatique et Météorologique de France formed.
	September 24th	Giffard airship makes its first flight.
1853		Cayley's man-carrying glider makes uncontrolled flight.
		Loup produces first French aeroplane design with airscrew.
1854	*June* 27th	Letur crashes while testing his parachute-glider and dies later.
1856		Carlingford designs monoplane in Ireland, and flies model as a kite.
		Le Bris commences gliding experiments.
		Mouillard tests gliders.
1857		Du Temple starts to experiment with clockwork-powered model aeroplanes.
1858		Wenham starts his gliding experiments to prove his aerodynamic theories.
1859		Cordner in Ireland tests his multiple man-carrying kite.
1860		Lenoir invents gas engine.
		Smythies designs his combination ornithopter and fixed-wing aeroplane.
1862		Start of balloon use in the American Civil War.
1863		D'Amécourt starts his helicopter model experiments, initially with steam, but later with clockwork propulsion.
		De la Landelle produces multiple airscrew helicopter design.

185

		Bouçart builds and tests a man-powered ornithopter.
		Jules Verne publishes his *Five Weeks in a Balloon*.
		Société Francais de Navigation Aérienne formed.
1864		Aeronautical journal, *L'Aeronaute*, founded.
		D'Esterno publishes his *Du Vol des Oiseux*.
1865		De Louvrié produces the first design for a jet-propelled aircraft.
1866		Aeronautical Society (later Royal Aeronautical Society) founded in Great Britain.
		Wenham lectures on his discoveries.
1867		Butler and Edwards publish their delta-wing jet aeroplane and rotor tip jet designs.
1868		Le Bris concludes gliding experiments.
		Bourçart tests ornithopter.
		Hunter proposes jet aeroplane with jet lift.
	June	First aeronautical exhibition held at Crystal Palace by the Aeronautical Society.
		Stringfellow tests new steam-powered model, without success.
		Kaufmann tests steam-powered ornithopter, without success.
1870		Pénaud begins his experiments, initially using twisted rubber propulsion for models.
		Trouvé flies blank cartridge-powered ornithopter model.
1871		Pénaud flies his 'planophore' inherently stable model.
		Wenham and Browning build the first wind tunnel.
		Household tests his glider in South Africa.
1872		Henlein flies airship powered by envelope's gas.
1873		Renard tests Wenham-type glider.
		Marey publishes his *La Machine Animale*.
		Brown commences tests with tandem-wing models.
1874	*July 9th*	De Groof killed while demonstrating his ornithopter at London.
		Du Temple's flying-machine makes first powered aeroplane take-off, but fails to sustain flight.
1875		Moy successfully tests his 'Aerial Steamer'.
1876		Pénaud designs and patents full-sized amphibian.
		Otto invents four-stroke internal combustion engine using petrol as fuel.
1877		Kress builds rubber-powered tandem-wing monoplane model.
		Dieuaide and Forlanini produce steam-powered helicopter designs.
		Melikoff proposes Wankel-type turbine engine, and proposes this for a helicopter model.
1878		British Army forms Royal Engineers balloon section at Woolwich.
1879		Tatin's compressed air-powered monoplane model flies.

Dandrieux tests his first 'butterfly' helicopter models.

Biot builds and tests the oldest surviving man-carrying flying machine, a glider.

Brearey's 'wave action aeroplane' model flies.

1881   Mouillard's *Empire de l'Air* published.

1883   Tissandier brothers test their electric-powered airship.

Montgomery starts to experiment with gliders in the United States.

1884   Renard and Krebs test their electric-powered airship, '*La France*'.

Mozhaiski builds full-sized aeroplane, using steam engine, and this makes a powered leap in Russia.

Phillips patents his first aerofoil designs.

Daimler invents lightweight and high speed petrol engine.

Parsons invents steam turbine.

1886   Jules Verne publishes his *Clipper of the Clouds*.

1888   Wölfert's airship flies with petrol engine power.

1889   Lilienthal publishes his *Der Vogelflug als Grundlage der Fliegekunst*.

Hargrave invents the rotary engine.

1890 *October 9th*   Ader's steam-powered '*Eole*' becomes the first full-sized aeroplane to take-off under its own power, but fails to sustain flight.

1892   Langley commences tests with steam-powered models.

Lilienthal begins gliding experiments.

1893   Phillips tests his steam-powered multi-wing model aeroplane.

Parsons builds and tests steam-powered helicopter.

Hargrave invents box-kite.

1894   Chanute publishes his *Progress in Flying Machines*.

July 31st   Maxim tests his steam-powered biplane, which lifts itself off its guide rails.

1895   Lilienthal flies first piloted biplane hang gliders.

Means commences publication of the *Aeronautical Annuals*.

Pilcher begins gliding experiments.

1896   Chanute commences gliding experiments.

Langley produces his first successful steam-powered models.

Tatin and Richet fly their successful steam-powered monoplane model.

August 9th   Lilienthal crashes while gliding, dies following day.

1897   Ader tests his '*Avion III*', without success, October 12th and 14th.

1898   Aéro Club de France founded.

1899   Wilbur Wright builds biplane kite to test wing-warping.

Hargrave visits England and lectures.

September 30*th* Pilcher crashes while gliding, and dies on 2nd October.

1900 Wrights fly their No. 1 glider at Kitty Hawk.

First Zeppelin flight.

1901 Wrights fly their No. 2 glider at Kill Devil Hills, near Kitty Hawk.

Langley flies petrol-engined model monoplane.

Santos-Dumont circles Eiffel Tower in airship.

Kress's floatplane capsizes while taxying in Austria.

Aero Club, later Royal Aero Club, formed.

1902 Wrights perfect technique on their No. 3 glider.

Ferber builds Wright-type glider.

Lebaudy brothers complete first practical airship, the 'Lebaudy I'.

1903 Jatho tests unsuccessful biplane.

October 7th Langley's 'Aerodrome A' crashes on take-off.

December 8*th* Langley's 'Aerodrome A' crashes again, on take-off.

December 14*th* Wilbur Wright crashes 'Flyer' on take-off.

December 17*th* Wilbur and Orville Wright make the first sustained powered flights in a heavier-than-air flying machine.

Index

Numbers in italics refer to illustrations

191

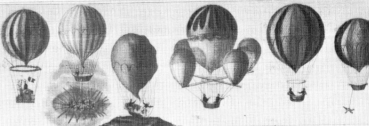

PREMIER VOYAGE AÉRIEN DANS UNE MONTGOLFI

THÉORIE

SYSTÈME PETIN